W9-BNY-075

THE CONGO

967.5
H

THE CONGO

A BRIEF HISTORY
AND APPRAISAL

by

MAURICE N. HENNESSY

FREDERICK A. PRAEGER, *Publishers*
NEW YORK

Wingate College Library

BOOKS THAT MATTER

PUBLISHED IN THE UNITED STATES OF AMERICA IN 1961
BY FREDERICK A. PRAEGER, INC., PUBLISHERS
64 UNIVERSITY PLACE, NEW YORK 3, N.Y.

All rights reserved

LIBRARY OF CONGRESS CATALOG CARD NUMBER 61–10034

To the boys and girls of Bedford
Rippowam School, who, although
their world is so far a cry from the
Congo, show such sympathy and
understanding for the Congo's
problems that it augurs well for the
Africa of tomorrow.

PRINTED IN GREAT BRITAIN

CONTENTS

A Map of the Congo will be found on pages 14 and 15.

18677

ACKNOWLEDGMENTS

I am most grateful to my wife Mary who has helped me over so many hurdles in the preparation of this manuscript, to my secretary Betty Brundage who wrestled so ably with the African names, to the Maryknoll Fathers for their help and the use of their library, to Mrs. Weiss of Katonah Library, to Frederick Waterman III for reading the manuscript and to Anne Farley, Paul Fisher, Moonyeen Cooper, Carolyn Wilson, and Peggy Braun of the United Nations, all of whom helped with the numerous chores that are part of writing even a short book.

INTRODUCTION

IN 1523, the grandson of a Congo king was raised to the Catholic episcopacy by Pope Leo X. He was the first negro south of the Sahara to be the recipient of such ecclesiastical dignity, and he was, indeed, the product of what has been called 'the Golden Age of Christianity' in the Congo. The king responsible for this hallowed era was King Nzinza Nkeuvu who was baptised in 1491 and whose kingdom stretched from Matadi to Kwango. So famous did the Congo become under his rule that the illustrious Portuguese poet, Camoens, in his *Lusiads* (v. 13) wrote : 'The greatest realm on these shores is that of the Congo.'

Towards the end of the nineteenth century, in this same 'greatest realm', there was not a single Christian; a few remaining crosses were worshipped as idols, cannibalism was rampant, while slavery with all its economic but vicious ramifications had ruthlessly destroyed the metaphorical, and had become the source of a material 'Golden Age'.

This kind of contrast happens, normally, once in the history of a nation; in the Congo it was to be repeated a second time but with much less fanfare and all within a period of 500 years. The word 'Christian' was to be replaced by 'industrial' and the Belgian nation took the place of a native ruler. While there were no spontaneous poetic pæans of praise, the Congo since World War II has been called the 'Tropical cornucopia'. Professor T. Wallbank of the University of Southern California wrote in 1954 that 'unrivalled in any other colonial area in Africa is the degree to which the native Congolese have been trained as skilled

artisans and technicians in the factories and the mines'. In
the same year William Uquex, editor of *La Cité Quotidi-
enne*, a journalist with an international reputation, said :
'Most travellers who cross Africa make the remark that
both blacks and whites in the Belgian Congo are active,
industrious and confident in the economic and political
system in which they collaborate.'

What of the Congo today? Just as Christianity collapsed
some three hundred years ago, so now have sanity, industrial development and harmony. A rudderless ship in a
raging storm is in no greater danger than this vast, flounder-
ing, leaderless territory where new-found freedom has
brought insecurity, fear, poverty and suffering in its wake.

Wherein lie the causes of the Congo's strange interludes?
This short book is an attempt to present the facts; it is for
the reader to draw his own conclusion.

M. N. HENNESSY

Bedford, 1961

CHAPTER ONE

THE DEVIL'S PARADISE

THE Portuguese discovered the Congo in the fifteenth century and built forts at the mighty river's mouth. They were first in the field, and had no cause to fear either economic or political rivalry on the West African coast from their European neighbours for at least a century. During this period of grace, they established a renowned Christian kingdom, exploited to a very limited degree the agricultural and mineral wealth of the country and in time introduced various fruits and plants from Brazil, as well as cattle from their own country, into what they hoped would be the garden of Portugal. Whether because their holdings all around the African coast were too extensive, or because too much wealth destroyed their adventurous and pioneering spirit, the Congo kingdom survived less than 200 years. While it lasted, it thrived in an aura of justice. Every time a Congo court assembled in Portuguese territory, the judge opened the proceedings with the words : 'Let not the money become black; let not Christ the Redeemer be overturned ! Speak but the truth; do not shame Christ. We, the chiefs, will not overturn the crucifix. We swear to deliver a just judgment.'

During this period in the Congo, the Portuguese must have witnessed a great artistic resurgence, which fostered in the Africans the desire to utilise great inherent artistic talent. The Congolese from the lower Congo basin produced some remarkable works of art which indicated a high degree of sensitivity and feeling and which are considered the finest art specimens in Central Africa. Even though Christianity

9

perished, some truly outstanding relics remained. An ivory tusk depicting the sixteenth-century reception of the white explorers is beyond price. And this is but one of a number of such relics, many of which indicate a deep religious fervour proportionate to their great artistic merit.

'Let not the money become black.' This warning was prophetic, but, as subsequent events showed, it went unheeded. The money from Africa did become black; in value, in terms of every business transaction, and as a mark against human behaviour.

The Portuguese Christian era was followed by the slave trade in all its viciousness, foster-father of so much human suffering and so much wealth. 'Black ivory' replaced money and for a period of nearly three hundred years the African continent, particularly its west coast, became a veritable devil's paradise. There had been slavery in Africa long before the white man came; but it had never been as lucrative as it was to become during the black years of the slave trade, nor had it ever been exploited to the degree that it was then.

Tribalism had always existed in Africa, but the slave trade gave it a fillip which was to intensify tribal hatred and promote constant warfare. Battles meant prisoners, prisoners meant slaves and slaves meant rum, geegaws and every other simple thing that appealed to simple, savage peoples.

While this nefarious business was ravaging the African coast, the Belgians neither had a nation of their own nor were they in a position to play any part in the Congo. The British started the slave trade and, just as soon as its economic potential became evident, the other European powers took a hand. Trade rivalry began in earnest. The Dutch, the French, the Danes and the Swedes all rushed in to participate in the human traffic and share in its enormous profits. The Americans, always on the lookout for a good deal, entered the field in the final years. Between the seventeenth and eighteenth centuries the British alone transported two million slaves. This meant that they must have picked up six million human beings for the death rate in transit was estimated at two in every three.

Just as the British were the pioneers of the slave trade, so were they the leaders in its abolition. Granville Sharp, Wilberforce and Hannah Moore, amongst many, organised the Committee for the Abolition of the Slave Trade. Eventually they saw their efforts rewarded by the Mansfield Judgment of 1772. This was followed by an Act of Parliament which abolished the business of human cargo in 1807. The other participating nations followed suit and outlawed the slave trade. By 1863, it had virtually ceased.

While many of the nations engaged in the slave trade were aware of the economic potential of the African coast, none of them had taken the time to explore its full possibilities. Cheap labour, so easily available and in such abundance, destroyed the incentive for exploration. Although for centuries ships had been sailing up and down the coast and following the courses of the Congo and the Niger for short distances, practically nothing was known of the African interior. Trading stations had been set up to facilitate the slave trade; others were established later to ensure its prevention. All these were confined to the coastal areas.

When it was realised that the abolition of the slave trade had brought the era of easy money to an end, there began a new clamour to push further into the African hinterland. The British again took the lead, and in 1788 Sir Joseph Banks, a noted English scientist, formed the African Association. His objective, framed in high-sounding language, was 'to promote the cause of science and humanity, to explore the mysterious geography, to ascertain the resources and to improve the condition of that ill-fated continent'. This association was followed by many others, all of which included in their avowed intentions beautiful phrases about Christianity, nobility and human dignity. They utilised Christianity as the excuse for further exploitation of the unfortunate African people. They did, however, have one positive result in so far as they instigated a period of real exploration into the African bush. Mungo Park, Livingstone, Stanley, Speke, Burton, and a number of others—some of whom were genuinely fired with Christian zeal—all began their intrepid journeys into the heart of Africa. Livingstone was one of the early pioneers in the Congo, where he was shortly followed by Stanley, of 'Mr. Livingstone, I presume' fame.

Stanley was the most remarkable explorer of them all. A Welshman by birth, he was endowed with the fiery Celtic imagination of his ancestors. In his early years he went to America, became an American citizen and worked for the *New York Herald*. Although Stanley is best known for his African journeys, he could easily have claimed fame in another field for he was a great journalist. He had travelled most of the known world for his newspaper and proved himself to be one of the truly remarkable reporters of his time. When, between the years 1856 and 1871, Livingstone disappeared into the African bush, the *New York Herald* sent Stanley to the Congo to find him. After searching for 236 days he succeeded. He found something else also—an entirely new career and one which was to change not only his own life but the whole course of African history.

So clamorous was the exploration and colonisation vogue that it was quite evident that trouble was just around the corner. The Portuguese (the original pioneers), the British, the Dutch and the French were particular rivals, and to such an extent that there was serious danger of open war.

Sitting back in Europe watching the whole performance was a man who was monarch of a nation itself less than fifty years old. He was Leopold II of Belgium. He was a man of inordinate ambition, and centred his designs on Africa and particularly on the Congo. Possibly he saw that, due to its geographical position, its narrow approach to the sea, and the particular mystery of its interior, the Congo basin had escaped much of the depredation of the slave trade. Probably he also realised that he stood less likelihood of opposition if he set his heart on this particular area.

In 1876 Leopold called a conference in Brussels to examine the African situation and, as he expressed it, 'to open
to civilisation the only part of our globe where Christianity
has not penetrated and to pierce the darkness which en-
velops the entire population'. Here again we find the
exalted language that was in reverse proportion to the
nobility of the real intent. As a result of this conference, an
International African Association was formed; very quickly
it became, to all practical purposes, the personal organisation of Leopold. The success of this move encouraged the
wily king to conceive another idea. He formed the International Association of the Congo. This he controlled
entirely and, as will be seen, to great effect.

While Leopold was looking to his own interests, the rivalry
for Africa became more intense. The saner participants
realised that the prize was too great to be lost by the risk of
war, and consequently, in 1884, a conference was called in
Berlin by Bismarck. Its purpose was to attempt to iron out
the differences between the nations with territorial ambitions
in Africa and at the same time to draw up a set of rules for
would-be exploiters which would prevent open conflict. Up
to this point the general pattern had been for each country's
exploration parties to push inland from the coast until they
met each other. They were then faced with the alternatives
of making a gentleman's agreement or fighting it out there
and then. The latter did not appeal very much in the bush,
especially as all concerned were fully occupied fighting
climatic conditions and the dread diseases of the tropics.
On the other hand, many of the gentleman's agreements
were of short duration and were by no means the kind of
pacts that were likely to stand the test of time or form a
firm basis for future peace. The conference at Berlin laid
down certain rules, heard and decided on the claims of
such nations as France and Portugal, and at the same time
produced the most high-sounding resolutions, couched,
according to pattern, in language as hypocritical as it was
inapt. The main safeguard against an all-out clash was a

Wingate College Library

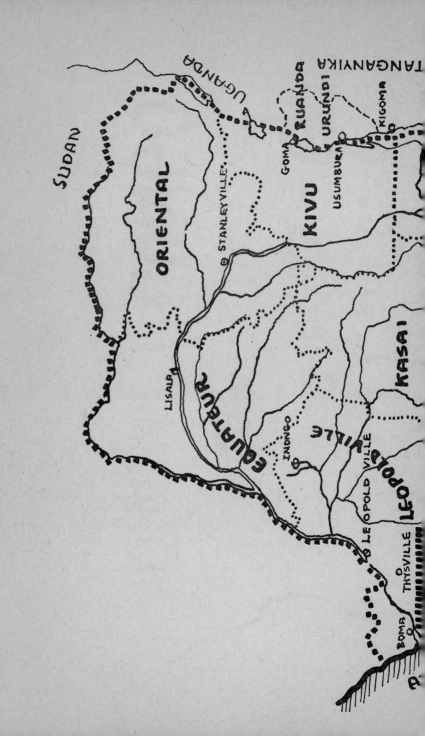

CONGO

The Republic of

P. K. FISHER JR.

TANGANYIKA

ELISABETHVILLE

SAKANIA

RHODESIA

KATANGA

KAMINA

DILOLO

ANGOLA

ATLANTIC OCEAN

unanimously approved resolution by the signatory nations that each nation should notify the others of its plans for colonisation, and at the same time outline the territories within which it proposed to operate.

One very important thing the conference did—and heaven knows how or why it did it!—was to recognise the rights of Leopold's Congo Association. This was, indeed, a very clever achievement on his part, for it established the legal basis on which this vast territory was eventually to become his own private back garden. He did, of course, know very little about it and we shall see how he decided to garden it.

Immediately following the Berlin Conference the exploration and exploitation of the African continent was pushed forward with enormous energy. During the next fifteen years, most of Africa came to be divided among six European nations—Britain, France, Germany, Italy, Belgium and Portugal. Arbitrary lines of demarcation were drawn through territories without any regard whatever for tribal or ethnological groupings or, indeed, for anything other than sheer expediency. These lines have since become the cause of much bloodshed and many heartaches, and have given birth to many of the problems which now trouble the United Nations. Whole peoples, like the Ewe people in Togoland, the inhabitants of the Cameroons and many others, were split down the middle and became subservient to different powers.

Leopold, however, carried out his purpose in an entirely different way. He sought out Stanley and asked him to become his agent in the Congo. Stanley, in the meantime, had been snubbed by his own people, probably because of what they considered his desertion to the United States. He was only too glad, therefore, to accept Leopold's offer, so that between the years 1879 and 1880 he undertook numerous journeys and made many speeches to the Congo chiefs, eventually obtaining some 900,000 square miles of territory for his master. In the early years, the other European nations were not concerned, although aware of Leopold's success in the colonial field. He appears to have excited remarkably little jealousy. His next door neighbour in Angola (Portugal), seeing the enormous inroads Leopold was making, became apprehensive and afterwards openly resented his terrific expansion, but too late to have any effect. As a signatory to the Berlin Agreement, there was little she could do but acquiesce—so Leopold was left to ravage at will his unfortunate Congo people.

CHAPTER TWO

EARLY DAYS IN THE CONGO FREE STATE

THE most surprising aspect of the Berlin Conference was that it agreed that the Congo should be the personal property of Leopold II. Less than three months later, on April 28th, 1885, the Belgian Parliament ratified this decision. The passing of the necessary legislation was unanimous, except for one dissentient. The text of the legislation was as follows : 'His Majesty, Leopold II, King of the Belgians, is authorised to be the chief of the state founded in Africa by the International Association of the Congo. The union between Belgium and the new State of the Congo shall be exclusively personal.'

Despite this amazing political decision, the Conference of Berlin tempered its magnanimity with certain regulations for the Congo basin. Their chief importance lies in the fact that they were, apparently, created to be disregarded; and when they were, they became the source of much dissension. The following constituted the main regulations :

1. The trade of all nations shall enjoy complete freedom.

2. All flags, without distinction of nationality, shall have free access.

3. All differential dues on vessels, as well as on merchandise, are forbidden.

4. No power which exercises or shall exercise sovereign rights in the above-mentioned regions shall be allowed to grant therein a monopoly of favour of any kind in the matters of trade.

It is really difficult to understand (unless, of course,

Leopold had completely deceived most of Europe) how it could ever have been a serious consideration that he intended to abide by these decisions. A monarch demanding that nearly a million square miles of territory should be his own personal property could scarcely be described as a philanthropist. His personal life was quite appalling; even that most charitable of documents, the *Encyclopedia Britannica*, has an entry which reads : 'Leopold was a man of notoriously immoral life.'

It is even more difficult therefore to understand how he could ever be referred to by historians as an 'impractical kingly philanthropist'. At the actual conference, Prince Bismarck said of him : 'All of us here render justice to the lofty object of the work to which His Majesty The King of the Belgians has attached his name; we all know the efforts and the sacrifices by means of which he has brought it to the point where it is today; we all entertain the wish that the most complete success may crown an enterprise that must so usefully promote the views which have directed the Conference.'

The French representative at the meeting said : 'The New State owes its origin to the generous aspirations and the enlightened initiative of a Prince surrounded by the respect of Europe.'

Apparently all the signatories were in complete agreement with these eulogies—a fact difficult of comprehension. Either most of those concerned were as hypocritical as His Majesty, or they were playing to one of the most naïve galleries in history. The signatory nations appeared to be in complete agreement.

The United States never really ratified the agreement, but on the other hand, they sent a plenipotentiary in the person of one Mr. Kasson. On December 10th, 1884, two weeks after the opening of the conference, this gentleman made a speech drawing a comparison between the intentions of the various powers in Africa and that of the Americans when they opened the West. In the course of his speech, he said : 'The present condition of central Africa reminds one much of that of America when that continent was first opened up to the European world. How are we to avoid a repetition of the unfortunate events, to which I have just alluded, amongst the numerous African tribes? How are we to guard against exposing our merchants, our colonies and their goods to these dangers? How shall we defend the lives of our missionaries and religion itself against the outburst of savage customs and barbarous passions?

'Finding ourselves in the presence of those whom we are urging to undertake the work of civilisation in Africa, it is our duty to save them from such regrettable experiences as marked the corresponding phase in America.'

In the light of subsequent developments in the Congo, prior to independence, and to still more recent events, this and the other speeches are of some importance. The most puzzling aspect of the United States' attitude was the lack of compatibility between the United States Government's refusal to ratify the Berlin Agreement and at the same time have its accredited representative make such a favourable speech. The explanation may lie in the fact—although there does not appear to be any distinct reference to it— that the United States Government did not agree with the Congo's becoming the personal property of the monarch.

Leopold retained control of the Congo Free State until 1908. In a statement addressed to Monsieur Beernaert, Belgian Minister of Finance, on August 5th, 1889, he made known his intention of willing the state to the Belgians. He wrote : 'I have therefore made, as Sovereign of the Independent State of the Congo, the Will that I send you. I ask you to communicate it to the Legislative Chamber at the moment which shall appear to you the most opportune.' He used the words 'most opportune' with a reason; he was about to ask for a loan of one hundred and fifty million francs and was really offering the Congo as a *quid pro quo*. The money was granted—a fact which proved that whatever else may be said, the monarch had the confidence of the Belgian people in the early days of the state just as he had of his colleagues at Berlin. This popularity was to wane considerably and, as we shall see, to be the cause of a major political crisis in Belgium when the time came for the Government to accept responsibility for the Congo state.

Hitherto the Congo had been run by men of various nationalities; the two chiefly responsible had been Stanley, the explorer, and Sir Francis de Winton. The latter had been an official of the International African Association and when Stanley returned to England from the Congo on June 10th, 1882, Sir Francis replaced him as head of the organisation's activities in the Congo. As soon as the King took over he appointed Monsieur Camille Janssen as Administrator General—a title which was later changed to Governor General. The town of Boma was made the administrative head of the state while a Vice-Governor was appointed for the Upper Congo.

In the early days Leopold made haste slowly. He even allowed English capitalists to promote a company and had a number of prominent Englishmen on his staff. The Administrator General, meanwhile, began to make re-strained but concentrated efforts to explore the resources of the vast territory. But money was scarce; at this stage funds had to be provided by Leopold himself. There were numerous other difficulties which required attention before the real task of economic exploitation could be undertaken. Despite the official abolition of the slave trade, it was still going strong. There were slave-trading strongholds firmly ensconced in strategic parts of the state; they were strongest at Manyema and looked as if they might become a real menace to progress. Strong Arab forces at Aruwimi and Lomami were even more of a menace, especially as they had perpetrated some appalling atrocities.

One of the first needs, therefore, was to form an army. This was done in 1897 by Baron van Eetvelde, who was

Secretary of State to Leopold II and was actively concerned with the material development of the Congo Free
State. It was he who concluded the famous treaty with the
United Kingdom in connection with the Cape to Cairo
Railway, which was the great ambition of Cecil Rhodes.
An interesting sidelight on the formation of this national
force was that, between 1883 and 1903, over eight thousand men came from the British West African forces in
Lagos, Accra and Sierra Leone. These were the British
colonial forces which were later amalgamated to form
the Royal West African Frontier Force. They had heard
through their own bush telegraph that the Congo was re-
cruiting soldiers; they drifted into the Congo having been
previously assured of a welcome by travellers who had gone
there. The original plan for forming the Congo State Force
was that annual levies of men should be imposed on the
chiefs. Service was for a period of five years with two years
on the reserve. The final decision on the selection of personnel was made by the local district administration.

As soon as some semblance of an army was ready and
partially trained, it was decided to subdue the Arabs and
destroy the slave trade. This task fell, for the most part, to
a Belgian named Baron Francis Dhanis.

The Arabs had as one of their leaders a native Congolese
named Gongo Luteta who appears to have been one of the
strongest elements in the Arab faction. Luteta had been a
thorn in the side of the early explorers. He had remarkable
qualities of leadership, and in an effort to maintain his own
prestige, he joined the Arabs. On March 15th, 1892, the
latter completely massacred a group of merchant adven-
turers. The response was an all-out attack on them, as a
result of which Dhanis defeated Luteta, who thereupon
became an ardent ally of the Belgians. (This action was not
uncharacteristic. During World War I an African sergeant-
major in the German army known as Charlie Maiduguri
won the Iron Cross for gallantry while fighting with the
Germans. Charlie joined the British when the latter

defeated the Germans in the Cameroons and ended up by
winning both the Distinguished Conduct Medal and the
Military Medal in the service of his original enemies!)

While getting rid of these various obstacles, limited exploration was carried out in the Congo. But there was still
much to be done. The high-sounding assertions made at the
conference were still fresh in the minds of all the participants but not to the extent that they gave any serious consideration to the fact that these high-sounding ideals were
being ignored.

In the southern region of the Congo Free State (as it
was known at that time) was Katanga, a name which has
become so very familiar during the past year. Situated between the Lomami and Lualaba rivers, it derived its name
from a local chieftain. Just as in Europe, so apparently in
the Congo, wise marriages were quite far-reaching in their
effect. Chief Katanga had a pretty daughter who married
an ivory merchant called Msiri—a man of outstanding
ability. In fact, he was so outstanding that in a matter of
seven years he became master of the whole area surrounding Katanga. He was as notorious as he was dynamic and
was, amongst other things, a slave trader. At one stage, his
power not only worried the Belgians in the Congo itself
but seriously alarmed the British in the neighbouring
territories.

In 1891, the *Compagnie du Katanga* was established to
exploit this new area and to act for Leopold in a military
capacity. The company was granted full ownership of one-
third of the state lands in the whole region; two-thirds was
to go to the King. Partially successful, the organisation
worked for the integration of Katanga with the Congo
state.* Although the latter had been ceded to Leopold by
the Berlin Act, both its slave trade operations and the unusual strength of its chief had caused it to be considered a

* With the signing of the Berlin Act, the Congo Free State came
into existence. It became the Belgian Congo when it was taken over
by the Belgian Government in 1908.

semi-independent territory. While this purpose was being pursued, a young English officer, Captain Stairs, undertook a special mission in connection with the project. His task was to ensure that Msiri became a loyal subject and stopped his marauding. The expedition cost Stairs his life; it also resulted in the death of Msiri and prepared the way for the final inclusion of Katanga as part of what has since been known as the Belgian Congo. On October 29th, 1906, the *Union Minière du Haut Katanga,* with a capital of ten million francs, was founded. This was the direct result of an Englishman, Mr. R. Williams, the friend of Cecil Rhodes. Williams had been given, previously, a five-year concession to prospect for minerals in Katanga. The enormous wealth which resulted from this institution was only to be realised at a much later date. It was also the reason for the construction of the railway linking the Congo to Rhodesia.

Although Leopold, from all appearances, had his hands full with his vast territory, he still had designs on areas outside his own boundaries. He was watched too critically by his colonial neighbours to have much success, but by an agreement, dated May 12th, 1894, Great Britain leased to the Congo the left bank of the Nile from Mahagi on Lake Albert in the south to Fashoda in the north, as well as the part of the basin of the Bahr-el-Gazal bounded by the twenty-fifth meridian on the west and the tenth parallel on the north. In this connection, Lord Cromer, who had visited the Sudan, made a significant comment when he said that 'on the Belgian bank of the Nile not a village or human being was to be seen, while the Anglo-Egyptian bank bore every sign of a contented and prosperous population'. As an explanation, he also wrote : 'The reason of all this is obvious enough. The Belgians are disliked. The people fly from them; and it is no wonder that they should do so for I am informed that the soldiers are allowed full liberty to plunder.'

CHAPTER THREE

THE CONGO SCANDAL

BETWEEN 1885 and 1908, Leopold II was the supreme legislative and executive authority in the Congo Free State; his form of government was, of necessity, unique. He had never seen the Congo, nor was he ever in a position where he was likely to do so. In the early stages, he endeavoured to run the Congo state from Belgium through an Administrator General. This arrangement put him in a very fortunate position for when trouble arose he was able to absolve himself from personal blame and attach it to his absent representatives.

Much power was vested in the Administrator General, but as there were no separate legal and executive bodies many quarrels, misunderstandings and difficulties ensued. As was inevitable, numerous changes in personnel and tactics took place before the country was divided finally into fifteen districts, each of which had a Commissioner representing the Administrator General. While this arrangement limited the areas controlled by representatives, it still did not prevent almost unlimited power being placed in the hands of individuals—individuals who were, often, the least suitable to exercise such responsibility.

Adopting an entirely different approach from the British, who operated mainly through existing chiefs, through whom they strengthened local authority, the Congo administrators began to reduce steadily the power of their chiefs. They divided the chieftaincies into zones and later, these zones into sectors. Many of the present problems, as we shall see later, stem from this disregard for existing institutions. The mere reduction of a chief to the level of an ordinary individual, although a contributory factor, was not the real danger created by this system. It was the fact that the whole native tribe was frequently left at the mercy of a local officer or, in some cases, an African menial who was likely to carry out quite ruthlessly any orders passed on to him. All too frequently these officials used their position to pursue personal interests, avenge feuds, and, at times, even levy their own private taxes. In matters of routine administration this was not so serious, but when the economic drive to exploit the resources of the country was put into gear, then it became the source of serious trouble. In the first place, an African had no rights. The European residents had only a few limited ones, but they had on their side the basic principle that in any dispute between African and European, the latter's word (the accepted one) was law. This gave rise to every kind of abuse, and it was not unusual to find a local officer flogging mercilessly, without any legal right, any individual African who failed to comply with his wishes. As was to be expected, with development came an increase in outrageous abuses.

The granting of concessions to various companies was a natural sequel to the kind of rule Leopold established and to his lust for wealth. In all cases, he ensured that a large part of any profits went to himself, but in order to foster this end, an abundance of labour was a primary requirement. Consequently, quite early on a system of work as a tax medium was initiated. Each chief was authorised to collect taxes; he did so by demanding that individuals should work for a specific period of time for a minimum payment. This, of course, was another name for slavery. The so-called taxpayers were treated like prisoners; their work was carried out under the supervision of armed sentries, and, as can be easily imagined, the system lent itself to all kinds of tyranny, brutality and subsequent reprisals by the natives. In one concession alone one hundred and forty-two Afri-

cans were killed. The spirit of bitterness and hatred gene-
rated in the people was quite terrifying, but little could be
done about it as there was not enough control in the area
to prevent the various agents from misusing their power.

In 1903, some effort was made to effect a remedy and
the so-called tax was fixed at forty hours of labour per
worker per annum. This attempt failed and so urgent was
the demand for money-making rubber that, if anything,
abuses increased. The unfortunate inhabitants were subjected to appalling suffering and fatigue. Frequently the
chiefs, whose power anyhow was almost nil, were arrested;
the women of the tribes were taken as hostages; the men
were flogged, and barbarism of all kinds became the rule
rather than the exception. Unhappily, little could be done
about it. The scarcity of administrators made it necessary
to invest legislative authority in the hands of commercial
agents. In most cases, this meant that the execution of
justice militated against the greed of the agents. The
result was obvious.

The material success of these companies can best be
judged from the fact that between 1893 and 1900 the
revenue rose rapidly from 5,500,000 francs to 26,000,000
francs; by 1901 it had become 31,000,000 francs. The two
main products responsible for this growth were ivory and
rubber.

In the meantime, rumours of the state of affairs in the
Congo were finding their way abroad. In England in particular, indignation began to grow and reached fever
pitch when a Captain Burrows, who had travelled in the
Congo, wrote a book describing some of the horrors which
he had witnessed there.* He was sued for libel by a Belgian,
Captain Henri Joseph Leon de Kayser. The case was one

* The manuscript for this book was entitled *The Congo Free
State*. A contract for its publication was signed between the
author, Captain Guy Burrows and R. A. Everett & Co., 42 Essex
Street, Strand, London, on November 17th, 1902, but as a result
of the libel case, it was never actually published, although its
contents were publicised widely in most parts of the world.

of the more celebrated judicial wrangles in the history of the British courts. The Belgian won his case and got five hundred pounds damages, but not before he had poured fuel on a flame of righteous anger which was to affect most of the civilised world. To treat in detail the arguments, enquiries, speeches and publications on the Congo scandal would fill many more pages than there are in this volume. There were, however, certain considerations which must be appreciated if some attempt is to be made to ascertain the truth.

Leopold II was remarkably successful and maintained in the early days a fair measure of confidence and respect in Europe despite the fact that he had relegated the platitudes of the Berlin Conference to the background. It was when he began to limit the activities of the free traders and to make it evident that there was little encouragement for any exploitation in the Congo other than that undertaken by those specifically appointed by himself (and these, for the most part, were Belgians) that he began to encounter real opposition. Consequently, it would be unwise to accept, *in toto,* Britain's wholehearted condemnation of the so-called atrocities in the Congo. Her motives were not entirely altruistic.

The British were not the only ones involved; the Germans were also keenly interested in the accusations. With their military background, they felt that the King had bitten off more than a small power such as Belgium was entitled to, much less an individual. The reason for their disapproval was quite evident.

An unfortunate incident aggravated the situation. A British subject, Mr. C. Stokes, was summarily executed by a Belgian officer called Lothaire for the alleged selling of arms and ammunition to Arab slave traders. Peculiar circumstances surrounded the killing. Lothaire had, apparently, invited Stokes to his camp under circumstances which the latter presumed to be entirely social. He accepted the invitation and was executed promptly.

Stokes was an employee of the German Government in

East Africa and had a number of natives with him when he visited the Belgian. Many of these were also killed, and the German Government immediately laid the whole matter before the British. To them the incident presented an opportune occasion to press further the campaign against the Belgian King.

In the meantime, Britain's imports from the Congo had fallen by two-thirds, while Congolese exports to Belgium had increased six-fold. This, of itself, was quite enough to make the idea of outrageous tyranny by the representatives of the Belgian King very palatable. The King's supporters, on the other hand, claimed that in the British, French and German territories there were also considerable suffering and tyranny quite equal to anything going on in the Congo. Certainly, they were right and if there was a difference, it was merely a matter of degree.

However, so strong was feeling in Britain that a Congo Reform Association was formed in Liverpool after the Burrows libel case. This body made numerous appeals to the United States and to a number of European countries to curtail Leopold's activities. The charges were of such a nature and were repeated so often that the whole affair became an international political issue—an issue which was to foster, among other things, fierce religious friction. Leopold was very close to the Catholic Church in Belgium and had given full support to its limited missionary activity in the Congo. It was not surprising, therefore, that the accusation against the Belgian King found little support from Catholicism in other parts of the world. Even in the United States, as we shall see subsequently, the Catholic hierarchy sided with the King of the Belgians and treated him as a great Christian benefactor instead of the roué he really was.

So fierce did the quarrel become that it forced the signatories to the Berlin Agreement to take a closer look at the document they had signed. For the first time, they realised the full significance of what had been agreed; none of the terms of the Berlin Agreement was in operation, nor had any attempt been made to implement them. The British House of Commons, in 1903, made an impassioned plea to the signatories to scrap the agreement and referred them 'to the system of forced labour, to the failure to effect anything for the moral welfare of the natives, to the fact that natives avoided contact with Belgian posts, and to the neglect by the State of the commercial clauses of the Berlin Act'.

Leopold's reply was as violent as it could be. Abuses by the British in Nigeria and in Sierra Leone were cited; in simple language, the British were told to mind their own business and clean up their own backyard. There was a not surprising lack of unity on the part of the other colonial powers to support Britain, for they were apprehensive of the growth of British colonialism and, at the same time, were not at all anxious to have their own misdeeds dragged into the light of world opinion. The United States did show some sympathy with the British point of view, but did not in any way appear anxious to interfere in a matter which might embarrass her, especially if reference was made to her own Negro situation.

A member of the New York Bar, Mr. Henry Wellington Wack, who had lived in England for a number of years and who had become a Fellow of the Royal Geographical Society, wrote a somewhat weighty volume on the issue.* He had, he believed, free access to all the documents in the Congo Administration Office, and in the preface to his book referred to an interview with Leopold in the following terms : 'His Majesty added that he had no fear but that the American people, when informed of the truth about the Congo, would appreciate, *as he did*, that the Congolese civilisation movement is the greatest colonising success in the history of the world.' Of the British, who were condemning the Congo misrule, he wrote : 'The smug men of the study, untravelled in regions wilder than Westminster, St. Albans or Liverpool, are as incompetent

* *The Story of the Congo Free State,* New York, 1905.

to judge of civilisation in Congoland as are the Manyema of the lack of it on Park Lane, in London.'

The strength of Mr. Wack's argument can best be judged from the fact that he had been no nearer the Congo than 'the smug men of the study'.

As a result of all the furore, the British Government sent Roger Casement to conduct, on its behalf, full enquiries. His subsequent report confirmed that there was a system of oppression in the area, that there was an organisation for forced labour, and that murder and mutilation were frequently the unjust punishment meted out to unfortunate Africans. The report added fuel to the fire. The Congo Reform Association demanded this time an international enquiry. It also called again for the cancelling of the Berlin Agreement and even had the temerity to suggest that British consuls should be appointed in the Congo to exercise jurisdiction.

Apart from the serious issues involved, the fact that Roger Casement* should have been the gentleman sent to conduct the enquiry adds considerable interest, in our day, to the whole affair. Casement, because of his part in the Irish Revolution of 1916, was hanged for treason. A little over a year ago, a bitter quarrel broke out between the Irish Government and Great Britain as to his personal documents. The Irish Government demanded them for their archives; the British Government intimated that Casement was a moral pervert, and altogether a thoroughly undesirable character and refused to hand them over. The logic of it all is not quite clear; but it was as a result of this man's report that Britain was almost prepared to go to war on account of the Congo affairs.

After much adverse publicity, accusation and counteraccusation, the King did agree to initiate reforms. Before they were to become a reality, there was to be considerable internal conflict in Belgium, as well as a general review of the whole Congo situation.

* Roger Casement was knighted in 1911.

Chapter Four

THE CONGO CHANGES HANDS

AS his reign was drawing to a close, it was evident to Europe that, in accordance with Leopold's will, the Congo would soon have to come under Belgian jurisdiction. It was equally evident that the vituperation and hatred which the conduct of Congo affairs had elicited would be passed along with it. There was the added fact that much of the money he had borrowed from the Belgian Government had not been repaid. It was little wonder then that the Belgian people and Government began to look on the Congo as a national nuisance rather than as proof of territorial aggrandisement.

Although the Belgian people may not have been aware of it, Leopold's financial embarrassment did not mean that the Congo was not paying off. Huge personal fortunes were being made there; not the last of these was the vast sum which found its way into Leopold's private purse. It did not last long; he was a prodigal spendthrift, and much of the scandal in Europe was provided by his many amours. His gifts to his mistresses, who were to be found in every major city in Europe, provided a salacious topic for constant speculation and gossip.

Apart, also, from his private life, the King showed that, as he became more involved with women, his financial integrity began to deteriorate. Despite the fact that he had bound himself by solemn agreement not to contract any loan without the consent of the Belgian Parliament, he borrowed five million francs from an Antwerp bank on the security of sixteen million hectares of land, which were to be forfeited if the loan were not repaid by June 30th, 1895. The loan, of course, was not repaid; Leopold's purse was empty, and naturally, the transaction became public property.

Financial and social pressure on Leopold became so strong that in 1894 he approached his ministers, who prepared a Treaty of Cession and presented it to the Belgian Parliament in January 1895. Disgusted with the whole situation, a strong group in the legislature started a violent campaign against taking over the Congo. The campaign was successful although it did necessitate the granting, very reluctantly, of a loan to the King, on the understanding that he would withdraw the treaty. This pleased Leopold because it gave him ready cash and at the same time prolonged the opportunity of still further exploiting the Congo for his personal gain. The loan, granted in 1895, was to be repaid in 1901 when the question of annexation was to be referred to Parliament again.

When 1901 came, the issue was more explosive than ever. By this time, there was little doubt in anyone's mind that serious crimes had been committed in the Congo and that the maintenance of the *status quo* was impossible. The King once more, with ill-advised arrogance, took shelter behind his absolute sovereignty in the Congo but the Belgian Government declared its right to annex the territory (a right strongly enhanced by the King's postponement of repayment of the loan). Thus for eight years, with periodic lulls, the argument went on.

In the meantime, Leopold initiated a number of reprehensible financial schemes which earned for him the contumely both of his own countrymen and people abroad. So strong, however, was his personality that, invariably, he managed to inveigle some of Belgium's senior ministers to join his schemes. One of the more notorious of these was the creation in 1907 of a fund called the *Fondation de Niederfullbach*, to which he presented shares in his Congo

investments valued at about forty million francs. He declared that the object of the fund, among other things,
was to spend twenty-six million francs to improve Belgium.
He really intended it, however, for his own use. The strange
thing was that Monsieur Renkin, one of the leading Belgian Ministers, was involved. Before Leopold could play
too much hanky-panky with the fund, the Belgian Cabinet
decided to suppress the *Fondation* by decree.

Finally, on October 18th, 1908, the annexation became
a reality. Twelve days later the Belgian Government
created a Ministry of the Colonies. The Congo Free State
had become the Belgian Congo.

Troubles were by no means at an end, however. The
Belgians hoped that annexation would allay the criticism
of Europe and act as a guarantee of suitable reforms in
the Congo. On the contrary, both the British Government
and that of the United States refused to accept anything
less than a full assurance that the terms of the Berlin
Agreement would be adhered to and that the exalted ideals
promulgated on that occasion would become a reality. At a
mass meeting at the Albert Hall, London, presided over
by the Archbishop of Canterbury, these demands received
enormous support, not only in Britain, but throughout
Europe and America.

At this stage, Leopold II died and was succeeded by
King Albert who had travelled in the Congo and had seen
at first hand the misdeeds of his predecessor. The British
Government, believing that he would prove more amenable to reason and able to get the backing of his ministers,
pressed its demands with growing intensity. They harked
back to the Berlin Agreement and pointed out that, despite
its pledges, neither traders nor missionary organisations
were yet able to obtain the land necessary for their busi-
nesses and spiritual enterprises. They recommended the
following reforms : (1) Relief of the natives from excessive
taxation. (2) The grant to the natives of sufficient land to
ensure their ability to obtain not only the food they re-

quired but also sufficient produce of the soil to enable them
to buy and sell as in other European colonies. (3) The
possibility for traders, whatever their nationality might be,
to acquire plots of land of reasonable dimensions in any
part of the Congo for the erection of factories so as to
enable them to establish direct trade relations with the
natives.

Realising that there was little alternative, and at the
same time conscious of the urgent need for reform, the
Belgians between 1910 and 1912 instigated a number of
improvements. These affected, particularly, ownership of
land and native labour, and although much hardship
remained, they did help to eradicate many of the evils of
Leopold's régime. The nature of the reforms is summarised
in the following paragraphs which provide an interesting
sidelight in view of Britain's own African land policy.

The proposed reforms, as outlined by Rappaport in his
Life of Leopold II, were : 'The land belongs to the natives
who, according to local custom and by Decree of September 14th, 1886, reside, build and labour thereon. The
Governor General of the District Commissary is em-
powered, in order to forward the art of building among
the natives and encourage them to new efforts, to show in
each village a one-storied building three times the size of
those they already possess or even, in our opinion, a still
larger one. This land may not be sold by the natives without consent of the Government.

'Every adult native who is able to work is put either
individually or in a group, into a taxation district. The
Governor General adjusts the amount of taxation in relation to the ability of the different districts to bear it, and
the stage of development of the natives. It may not be
under six or over twenty-four francs a year. The tax is
payable monthly; under certain circumstances it may be
delayed. The native may pay it in produce or in work. The
number of hours of work must, under no circumstances,
exceed forty per head per month.

'A black under fourteen years of age cannot bind himself to a term of service of more than two years as an ordinary worker or of more than three years as errand boy or messenger.'

When these reforms were adopted, Lord Delamere, the East African pioneer, had already bought the White Highlands in Kenya from the local chiefs. The Belgians, possibly as a gesture of 'what you can do, I can do', also embodied in their regulations the right of chiefs to sell land. But even taking these two facts into consideration, there appeared to be considerable confusion—deliberate or otherwise—about the land issue in Africa.

But in their West African territories the British did not permit a chief to sell tribal land to Europeans—a fact which, more than anything, helped the easy transition to independence in Ghana and Nigeria. This divergence in policy tends to confirm the view that Britain had territorial ambitions in the Congo—a fact she never admitted openly during the days of the scandal. However, years after Leopold's escapades had been forgotten in the light of more startling events, further proof was forthcoming, as we shall see, of this African ambition.

Chapter Five

SOWING THE SEED

THE years immediately preceding the First World War were years of consolidation for the colonial powers. Affairs in Europe were of such a nature as to demand the attention of most of the nations with colonial interests. Consequently, the African territories were granted a period comparatively free from interference and squabbling.

The reforms in the Congo appeared to be lessening the burden of the natives; their effects were evident in numerous ways. Some of them even appeared at the time to bring considerable blessing; subsequently, as we shall see, they were to be the source of considerable trouble.

On the social side there was greatly increased activity in the religious field. The Protestant and Catholic missions had become active during the latter years of Leopold's reign; later they were joined by many other and various missionary organisations. The Belgian monarchs were Catholics, Belgium was almost ninety per cent Catholic, so it was to be expected that Catholicism should receive the most encouragement and assistance from the Belgian Government. There was also the fact that the Vatican had rallied to the defence of Leopold during the Congo scandal —a loyalty which paid handsome dividends. By a decree of Pope Leo XIII, Catholic priests working in the Congo were permitted to assume a civil status and, as a result, were paid salaries by the colony. This did not happen in the case of other religious organisations—a fact which was afterwards the cause of much dissatisfaction and abortive haggling. Practically the whole field of education became the responsibility of the missionaries and, indeed, after a short time the Roman Catholic Church became the real educative authority in the Congo.

With regard to land, despite all the resolutions which had been made, the basic concept established during this period was that collective ownership was the best system. Individual tenure was not altogether acceptable, although, under certain conditions, it was permissible. One matter of social importance was clarified and deserves special mention. By an Ordinance of November 23rd, 1912, the sale and delivery to natives, or the possession by them, of distilled alcoholic liquors was strictly forbidden (the introduction of absinthe, as a drink, had already been outlawed in the territory). This Liquor Act was one of the more welcome pieces of legislation, particularly as it enabled the Africans to protect their own interests and to avoid the frequent tribal quarrels which resulted in much bloodshed. This was supplemented by an international agreement signed on July 22nd, 1908, by which the United Kingdom, France, Portugal and Spain undertook not to deliver to the natives of the Congo, firearms, ammunition, or gunpowder. This agreement, while signed with the hypocritical avowal that it was a protective measure for the Africans, was in effect a defensive measure of considerable benefit to the European colonial powers.

This period saw great strides in the development of communications between the Congo and its neighbours. Katanga was bound to Rhodesia by a railway from Sakania to Elizabethville. A line was constructed from Katanga to Dilolo, the point on the frontier reached by the Portuguese railway from Lobito Bay. Internally a route by rail and water from the Katanga to the Congo mouth was completed; this meant over 800 kilometres of railway and nearly 3,000 of rivers. A postal service linking the Congo with the outer world was also set up. This was quickly followed by telegraphic communication. In the meantime, the three ports in the Congo—Banana, Boma and Matadi—had come to be served by four shipping companies, one Belgian, one French, one German and one British.

On the industrial side, rubber and ivory continued to remain the chief sources of income in the Congo proper. In Katanga, however, where real mineral wealth abounded, a new era of development was set in motion. The *Comité Special du Katanga*, to which reference has been made previously, was active in this operation although the Government took a hand with legislation. Prospectors were issued permits for two years on payment of a hundred francs. Should actual exploitation follow as a result of the prospecting, the *Comité* received one-third of all profits as well as five per cent annually of the gross value of the product of the mine.

During this period there was little legislation of an industrial nature, with the result that frequent quarrels arose with regard to trademarks, patents and the like. Labour still came within the province of government regulation and Africans still had to work either as a direct *corvée* or in lieu of taxation. The recruitment of labour underwent various legal changes; some of these are of interest. For example, a person could not be forced to work more than ten kilometres from his house. A married woman could not work without the permission of her husband. A student attending school by the direction of the state had to obtain the permission of his tutor if he wished to work. Wages had to be paid in actual cash monthly, and the employers, in many instances, had to house and feed their employees. During the period of a labour contract, the employer had to give an African labourer four days' leave a month, provide for him in illness for a period of fifteen days and repatriate him on the termination of the contract. These were indeed great changes from the early days of Leopold's exploitation.

It was during this period also that the foundations were laid for what were commonly called the colonial policies. Despite the fact that these represented the supposed wishes of a large proportion of the people in Europe, the average European knew very little about them; much less did he understand their basic differences. It is little wonder, therefore, that in the United States there was almost complete and utter ignorance about the various facets of colonialism. There was, however, one big difference : in government circles in Europe the various colonial attitudes were thoroughly understood; in America there was almost as much ignorance at the official level as there was amongst the masses. The American concept of colonialism was born of the spirit of Valley Forge, and the lack of foresight of George III when he precipitated the quarrel with the thirteen colonies. It was strengthened through the years by a long succession of Irish immigrants who, by their outstanding oratorical ability, reached high political office and who fostered and spread on all possible occasions their inherent hatred of Britain's 'colonialism'. In fact, the latter became synonymous with imperialism and imperialism just meant Britain. Until a few years ago, people in the United States rarely if ever associated colonialism with any nation other than Britain.

There might have been a change of attitude and a period of enlightenment but for the two world wars and the intervening depression which so occupied the minds of most people on both sides of the Atlantic that they spared little thought for the problems of colonial Africa. Belatedly, this attitude has now undergone a change—a change which, had it occurred years ago, especially in the United States, might have changed the course of Congo history.

It is advisable before studying the Congo position further to understand both the Belgian colonial policy— or the lack of it—and that of the other powers.

Britain's colonial system has been referred to frequently as the dual mandate, or the policy of indirect rule. The latter was devised and practised by Lord Lugard at the beginning of the century when he was in Nigeria and, due to its comparative success, was recognised as the prototype for all British colonial administration in Africa. It was based on the idea that each colony should, as far as possible, make its own laws, manage its own administrative and financial affairs, and do all this through the existing native institutions. This meant, on the economic side, that financial gain would result both to European investors and to the Africans themselves and that all the effort put into the development of the country would benefit both parties as long as they worked together. In countries where there were no land problems, such as Nigeria and Ghana, this system worked admirably and was to a great extent responsible for the peaceful progress to independence of these two territories. However, in places such as Kenya, where the Europeans have all the better land, the system does not operate so well.

One aspect of British colonial policy was of vital importance; it did, without question, envisage independence for the various territories in the future. No specific date for independence was, however, mentioned, or even envisaged, and this was to become one of the major problems of the future.

The French, with their vast territories, had their own particular attitude towards their African empire. The conquest of Senegal took place between 1854 and 1865, at a time when Napoleon III was ruling France under an absolute autocracy; this did much to shape future policy in the French colonial territory—a policy which was, naturally, moulded along the same arbitrary lines. What was done in Senegal provided the model for later additions to French colonial possessions. The natives were allowed to retain their old traditional laws and customs for the regulation of their own affairs so long as they did not conflict with the French governmental aims. As soon as they did, they found themselves treated as mere subjects and nothing else. However, while the French did not visualise that these countries would become independent territories, they did have the long view that in time they would all become a part of a French Union. This, they believed, would be achieved when the Africans attained a standard of education and culture which conformed to the French way of life.

Although the German influence in Africa was short-lived, its policy, because of the ultimate fate of its territories, is worthy of mention. All power was concentrated in the hands of German officials who ignored the indigenous peoples completely—tribes, chiefs, customs, traditions. In typically Prussian fashion, the Africans were treated as conquered subjects of the German Empire, and as a result had no legal rights. Germany lost her territories after the First World War and a later chapter will outline their distribution under the aegis of the League of Nations.

With regard to the Belgians, we have seen that initially there was no question whatsoever of any other motive than the economic exploitation of the whole Congo area. It was obvious from the beginning that the Congolese were treated as a subject people of a low category enjoying virtually no privileges or rights. This attitude was to remain, despite the reforms, until, as we shall see, there developed in later years the policy known as 'paternalism'; this term was really adopted to indicate that the Belgians were for-mulating some kind of positive attitude towards the native peoples.

Although the Belgian Government was consolidating its position, a new shadow had begun to loom over the Congo horizon—a direct counterpart to the dark war clouds gathering in Europe. It came from Germany which had long desired a foothold in the Congo.

It had been evident for some time that Germany was thoroughly dissatisfied with the extent of her African territories. These were, in the west, the German Cameroons, Togoland and South-West Africa. Her real ambition was to build a great German empire in central Africa. At one stage it looked as though she might gain a strong foothold —by peaceful means—from which she could move forward to further territorial gains. In 1912 there were many Belgian government officials who considered that the 900,000 square miles of the Congo territory were much too large, and that Belgium should sell part of them to Germany, France and the United Kingdom. There is little evidence available as to what stage these negotiations really reached, but it would seem that affairs in Europe galloped ahead too quickly and too unexpectedly for the overall German plan to reach fruition; at any rate, hostilities broke out before any definite agreement had been reached. From Africa's point of view this was fortunate, for war found the Germans unprepared for large scale military operations in that continent. In a later chapter we shall see the results of this unpreparedness.

CHAPTER SIX

BETWEEN THE WARS

WITH the cessation of hostilities in Europe, and the formation of the League of Nations, the disposition of Germany's colonies in Africa assumed high priority. The Belgian Congo and the dreams of a Central African Empire which, according to many politicians and students of international affairs, it fostered in the German mind, had constituted one of the main causes of World War I. Defeated Germany still demanded the retention of some of her colonies in Africa; the other colonial powers were divided on the issue. Altogether, it was evident that the problem of Africa was one which was likely to require much attention. Even at that time, there were many who foresaw that unless Africa was removed from the field of the international territorial scramble, it would be a constant menace to world harmony. In August 1917, H. G. Wells declared that the permanent peace of Europe was dependent on leaving access to the raw materials of Africa open to all.

For a long time, Britain had had ambitions in the Congo; British business interests had helped to exploit the mineral wealth of Katanga, despite the fact that in doing so they had, to all intents and purposes, made themselves industrially subservient to the Belgian Government. On this basis alone, many people restated the British claim to the Congo and dragged out of the bag the time-worn argument that the transfer of the Congo from Leopold II to the Belgian Government had, in effect, been an illegal procedure. It was suggested that the whole of the Berlin

Act should be reconsidered and that the League of Nations, or some similar body should re-examine all the African territories instead of merely disposing of the ex-German ones.

Many of the economic grievances of Britain were aired during this period. For example, France was severely criticised for preventing any nationals, other than French nationals, from exploiting French West African territory. The German apologists maintained that it would be in the interest of lasting peace to concede a part of the Congo to Germany. The German record in Africa, however, was such that there was little sympathy for this particular claim. The reason advanced for most of these claims was that the Belgian Congo was not, despite the reforms, being administered satisfactorily. There was one group in Britain which adopted the attitude that since Sir Roger Casement had been the man who revealed the atrocities in the Congo, and since he had been hanged for treason anyhow and was a friend of the Germans, his report must have been made in pursuance of German ambitions.

One of the most interesting aspects of this international bickering was that the Labour Party in Britain, in August 1917, issued its own particular memorandum* declaring that the real requirement with regard to Africa was an authority which should be recognised by all the belligerents and by every other independent state in the world. The memorandum contained the following statements : 'With regard to the colonies of the several belligerents in tropical Africa, from sea to sea (north of the Zambesi river and south of the Sahara desert), the conference disclaims all sympathy with the imperialistic idea that these should form the booty of any nation, should be exploited for the profit of the capitalist, or should be used for the promotion of the militarist aims of governments. In view of the fact that it is impracticable here to leave the various peoples concerned to settle their own destinies, the conference

* *Memorandum on War Aims. The Times,* August 11th, 1917.

suggests that the interest of humanity would be best served by the full and frank abandonment by all belligerents of any dreams of an African empire; the transfer of all the present colonies of the European Powers in tropical Africa, together with the nominally independent republic of Liberia, to the proposed supernational authority or League of Nations herein suggested; and their administration by an impartial commission under that authority with its own trained staff, as a single independent African state, on the principles of (1) the open door and equal freedom of enterprise to the traders of all nations; (2) protection of the natives against tribal interests; (3) all revenue raised to be expended for the welfare and development of the African state itself; and (4) the permanent neutralisation of this African state and its abstention from participation in international rivalries or any future war.'

Another advanced suggestion that prefaced the final disposition of the German territories by the League of Nations was that of neutralisation. This idea fostered the thought that Africa should come under the jurisdiction of an International Commission and that, as far as possible, there should be no interference by any specific European nation. On the other hand, this policy advocated that all nations should be free to trade in Africa. In the light of modern events, it is clear that after World War I there was wise thinking on Africa and that there were those who realised that it could easily be the source of world conflict. The idea of neutralisation, however, found little support; the strength of the lobbying by those involved industrially in Africa was much too great. General Smuts declared at the League of Nations : 'Nothing, indeed, can be more Utopian than to imagine that the effort to govern such an area by a commission would be productive of anything save the greatest amount of friction, leading inevitably to renewed war.' Even the question of freedom of trade in the Congo sparked a fresh frenzy of industrial indignation, and once again after forty years the Berlin Act became the subject of very serious study.

One other important and highly inflammable issue arose at this stage—and this for the second time. It was the question of missionary activity and education in the Congo. It had already been established (as we shall see in a subsequent chapter) that Roman Catholicism was to be one of the predominant factors in the Congo's development; as such, it was the recipient of special government favour. The post-war settlement was considered a suitable opportunity for demanding that equal rights should be offered to all religious denominations. Arthur Keith in his book, *The Belgian Congo and the Berlin Act,* said : 'It would seem desirable, therefore, to enact that any favour given to one religious denomination by the state must be equally available to any other on the same conditions, a decision which would have the result of tending to eliminate competition between religious denominations for the favours of the state, a process disadvantageous alike to religion and to the state.'

It was suggested at the same time that an international council should be set up, not merely to discuss these religious issues, but to advise on all manner of native problems and trade questions. However, most of these suggestions met with little success. With regard to the religious one, instead of Catholicism being weakened it seemed to grow in strength, especially in the field of education. In 1925, the Belgian Government introduced legislation which granted a monopoly of all government financial aid to education* to the Catholics for a period of twenty years. This caused a natural enough furore amongst the other missionaries and although they did eventually receive some aid, it was not until after the twenty years had elapsed and, then, it bore no relation whatever to the amounts received by Catholicism. This particular action of the Belgian

* Congolese education at this time was very restricted, and did not go beyond the primary level.

Government had far reaching effects which still influence greatly the Congo's destiny, for the relationship between Catholicism and education in the Congo is now considered to be a major reason for the present crisis.

Apart from the political, economic and social crises which the aftermath of war brought to the Congo, an entirely new one added to the general confusion. For the first time it was realised that African troops, properly trained by European standards, constituted a formidable fighting machine. The Belgians fought in the Cameroons, as, indeed, did the Nigerians; the Gold Coast troops fought in Togoland; in fact, an African sergeant-major in the Gold Coast was reported to have fired the first shot of the war in 1914. When the Germans were driven from West Africa, Belgian and Gold Coast and Nigerian troops participated in the struggle. This was significant, particularly since many of these soldiers enjoyed for the first time, contact with Africans other than their own fellow countrymen.

The real significance, however, of this experience with African troops was that they enhanced considerably the strategic importance of colonial territories. To the imperialists they presented a great reservoir of manpower for any future war; this of itself was a contributory factor to the problem of dividing out the territories among the belligerents.

After all the squabbling and futile wrangling, the League of Nations finally decided to allot Germany's west and central African territories to Britain, France and Belgium. Togoland was split down the middle in arbitrary fashion; Britain and France were each to administer part of it. The Cameroons received the same treatment and was to be administered in a similar manner. Ruanda Urundi, frequently called the Switzerland of Africa, was handed over to Belgian administration. At one time this area consisted of two distinct territories. It had a population density a hundred times greater than that of the Congo; it was situated in the north-eastern part of the territory. South-west Africa was handed over to the Union of South Africa.

It is one of the paradoxes of this contrary world that up to the moment the only one of these territories that has not caused serious disturbance in Africa is Ruanda Urundi, despite the fact that it is so close to the Congo. There are many who will say that the reason for this is that the Belgians, in accordance with the general lines of their colonial policy, made no attempt to kindle any kind of political or administrative ability in its inhabitants. On the other hand, Togoland, the Cameroons and South-west Africa have provided a long succession of troubles since the last war.

With the final disposition of these territories, Africa settled down again into a reasonably peaceful state. The cost of the war in Europe had bankrupted most of the nations, and Africa was looked upon as a potential source of recompense for the belligerents. That it was inhabited by people who had a vested interest in human rights was a thought that rarely entered people's heads, despite the fact that prior to the final decision by the League of Nations the world was subjected to the same hypocritical verbosity which had characterised the Berlin Agreement. However, so far as the Congo was concerned, one event of importance did occur; the Belgian administration firmly established its pattern of control. The territory was, to all intents and purposes, utterly and completely controlled from Brussels, although, strangely enough, more power was vested in the Belgian Governor General than in any of the British or French Governors. The British administrator has always had to cope with the Colonial Office despite the fact that the latter piously affirmed that it left decisions to the man on the spot. What it failed to state, however, was that it left the decisions to the man on the spot in order that he might afterwards be the victim, if things did not work out well. District commissioners were appointed in the Congo, their duties broadly similar to those of their counterparts in the British territories. Also as in British territories, there were touring officials, constantly visiting the different areas.

During these years, big business developed to an enormous degree, and five industrial giants literally controlled the country. They were, (1) Brufina (*Société de Bruxelles pour la Finance et l'Industrie*), which controls the Banque de Bruxelles and various industrial organisations; (2) Cominière (*Société Commerciale et Minière du Congo*), which ties in with the Nagelmackers financial interests and has huge agricultural properties; (3) Unilever (through its Belgian subsidiary, Huilever); (4) the Banque Empain, with strong interests in transportation and much else; and (5) the fabulous organisation known as the *Société Générale de Belgique*.

One of the more illuminating aspects of the operation of these organisations was that in nearly every case the Belgian Government in Brussels had almost a fifty per cent interest. The Government, therefore, not only received taxes from the companies, but also shared their dividends.

Although the apparent lot of Africans was much better, they still enjoyed few rights. Between the two wars, Belgian policy was clear cut; Africans belonged to a different world and were to be kept far removed from anything that savoured of European contact. Education, only in so far as it enabled them to carry out the rather lesser artisan tasks, was frowned upon. In fact, there was no secondary education nor, at that time, was it the intention that there should be any. The Belgians appeared to have created the ideal cultural compound, and it is a matter for considerable speculation whether they would ever have left it if World War II had not overtaken the world.

CHAPTER SEVEN

THE CONGO IN TRANSITION

THE Second World War marked the beginning, as well as being the cause, of Africa's great transition—a transition which is still gathering momentum. There was scarcely an area throughout the continent that in some way or another was not affected by the conflict. Many great battles were fought in North Africa, there was heavy fighting in Abyssinia, and the largest expeditionary force in the history of the British colonial empire left Africa to fight on other shores. Freetown harbour in Sierra Leone became one of the vital strategic ports of the Western world, and air bases along the west and east African coasts became essential to the air fighter supply to North Africa when the Mediterranean was closed to Allied shipping.

It was on the economic side, however, that the real change took place in Africa. Almost overnight, it became the great reservoir from which were drawn the most essential raw materials necessary for victory. From the Belgian Congo came the most important of all the raw materials—uranium. Without it the atomic bomb could not have been manufactured, nor could the Japanese have been brought to heel as speedily as they were. The story of the development of the Congo's uranium mine at Shinkolobwe belongs elsewhere, as does, indeed, that of Edgar Sengier, the man responsible for it. Their saga has been for so long wrapped in necessary secrecy that when it is written, it will be one of the more intriguing documents in international affairs. The main point, however, is that the Congo produced the uranium and, by doing so, projected itself into a position of world importance. This, in turn, attracted thousands of travellers, technicians, and personnel necessary to produce this most important raw material, vital to a changing and scientifically alert world. Nor was uranium the only commodity that gave prominence to the Belgian Congo; it also produced large quantities of rubber (in scarce supply owing to the loss of Malaya) and other strategic minerals.

The Congo also made its own military contribution, for it stationed a native expeditionary force in Egypt, the Middle East and Burma.

There were other factors which fostered change in the Congo as well as in many parts of Africa. The need for European personnel to command the great African armies became acute. Consequently, it was necessary to recruit for military service large numbers of trained administrative officials who had been in constant touch with the African peoples. These men were the advisers, guardians and general mentors of the men in the bush and constituted the very backbone of colonial government.

The expansion of the armies themselves brought thousands of men in from the bush. They came, wearing the minimum of clothing, and with little or no knowledge beyond that gleaned within the very narrow environs of their village life. They made contact for the first time with their fellow Africans, and for many it was the first opportunity to exchange ideas with men outside their own districts. This was a little appreciated but vital factor in fostering the great change in Africa. In our Western civilisation we have become so accustomed to radio, television and the cinema that the art of conversation, especially as a source of pleasure, has almost faded into insignificance. For centuries it has been the African's chief means of enjoyment, quite apart from being a medium of communication. Consequently, this wonderful opportunity for exchange of ideas was something which introduced a whole new world into the African mind. Its effect has too long been underestimated, especially by those whose knowledge of the African is derived from books or from very limited contacts.

War brought another interesting change, for in Ghana, Nigeria and East Africa, where hundreds of thousands of Africans became soldiers, it was the mandatory task of all officers to talk and explain to them the purpose of the war, to endeavour, in simple language, to outline the democratic system, and to show that its salvation was the main objective of the conflict. The Belgian Congo troops also experienced this, although their participation, at times, was more vicarious than direct. A whole regiment of the Congolese Army went to Nigeria during World War II and participated in exercises with the Nigerian, Ghanian and Sierra Leonean troops.* It was a strange fact that these soldiers, who had lived literally thousands of miles apart, were able to communicate with each other. There were difficulties but, somewhere along the way, there was always a dialect which became a medium for conversation or 'good talk'. This applied to the meetings of all African troops, no matter what their country of origin.

There were other activities which played an important part in the Congo's change. Flogging was permissible in the Congo Army and was, in fact, administered at a daily parade. Offending soldiers were treated exactly like children and had to take their punishment in the presence of their colleagues. When any weakness, suggestive of lack of courage, was displayed by an offender in the acceptance of punishment, it was normal for a senior non-commissioned officer to receive the flogging on his behalf. The purpose of this was to give a display of soldierly qualities befitting such an occasion. Amongst the British and French forces at this time, the striking of an African soldier, for any reason, meant court martial. The Belgian troops quickly

* The author served with the Belgian Congolese Army during this period and was attached to them while they were participating in tactical exercises in Northern Nigeria.

became aware of this and made an unfavourable comparison
with their own conditions, which later fermented great
hatred of Belgian colonialism.

A serious ill effect of war was the lowering of European
prestige in the Congo. The government officials who were
drafted into the army were all too often replaced by men
of lower calibre—a misfortune experienced in most African
colonies. All too often, the Africans, who normally enjoyed
European guidance, were left to themselves or found themselves, when in difficulty, in the hands of unsympathetic
officials. The Belgian Congo suffered particularly in this
respect, so much so that years after the war the Belgians
claimed that it was one of the major reasons for many
adverse changes. Guy Mallengreau, a professor at the
University of Louvain, said in Washington, in 1954* : 'The
bitterness on the part of the natives at this time was the
sharper since, being no great individualists, they had
difficulty accepting solitude and abandonment. "The
whites don't like us any more," they were saying after the
war; and the administration, knowing how easily hatred
can spring from confidence betrayed, looked uneasily on
the strangely unsmiling faces of the negroes.'

The war also produced another aid to Belgian reversal
in the Congo. The enforced statutory labour which the
demands of war necessitated started a big exodus from
the rural areas into the towns. In 1939, Leopoldville had a
population of 40,000; by the end of the war, it was 100,000;
and today it is over 300,000. This forced the Belgian
Government to think anew about their urban communities,
especially as organised unionism developed as a natural
result of the influx.

The African is a great imitator. Little wonder then that
when the large native population of Leopoldville realised
that the European workers in the city had unionised, they,

* Speech to the Conference on Contemporary Africa, sponsored
by the Johns Hopkins University School of Advanced International
Studies, August 1954.

too, demanded a union. The Belgians, with both wisdom
and foresight, realising that such a movement was inevitable, offered to help instead of opposing the Africans'
wish. In doing so, however, they adopted a paternalistic
attitude of tolerant benevolence, rather than allow real
power to seep out into African hands. At no time were the
unions in a position to take any such serious action as a
strike on their own behalf.

From all this it will be gathered that in the immediate
post-war years the Belgian Government had to apply itself
assiduously to mending the breaks in its cultural compound.
Conscious also that there were vital changes taking place
all around their African territory, the Belgians were quite
determined that their basic policy toward the Africans
should in no way undergo serious change. They saw the
ideal remedy in a change of economic conditions, which
would bring material satisfaction to the Africans and,
as they thought and hoped, destroy anything suggestive
of serious intellectual development among the natives.
Belgium itself was in a precarious economic situation
following World War II, so that the Belgian people as a
whole were in no mood to start thinking magnanimously
about the Congolese. This was understandable in view of
the great suffering German occupation had inflicted on
them. The Congo, in fact, was looked upon as the main
remedy for the many Belgian economic ills. The Belgian
Government, aware of the problems in the Congo, decided
to put both the Belgian and Congo ills under what has
become a traditional economic umbrella—a ten-year plan.
This one was planned in 1949 and put in motion in 1950.
It provided for new financial investment in the Congo
amounting to fifty billion francs, half of which was to come
from the Belgian Government and half from private investment. Transportation, electric power stations, scientific
equipment and public services, improved education and
hygiene were all part of the plan. The extension of tenant
farming was one of the more important projects. This was

aimed at reversing the great exodus from the rural areas; it was thought that the new system would persuade existing farming communities to remain where they were and tempt, by 1965, the return of 450,000 native families back from the towns to the land. Mechanisation and fertilisers were two of the attractions offered to the Africans in order to lure them back. These, they were asssured, would offer a standard of living equal to that of dwellers in urban communities.

The development of the Congo's river system was another projected undertaking, as was the improvement of the harbour installations. Modern roads were to be built, while asphalt-covered highways were to connect the east and west from Kivu to the Congo river.

An important aspect of the ten-year plan, and one which showed that the Belgians had begun to see the need for treading lightly, was that it contained no coercive implication of any kind. The goals set did not appear to be rigid, although it was evident that one basic thought was uppermost in the minds of those who had prepared it—a very considerable raising of the African standard of living.

The original investment in this plan came mainly from Belgium, the Belgian Congo itself, Switzerland, the United States of America and the International Bank for Reconstruction and Development. The Belgians set up no special administrative organisation to handle it; they entrusted its execution to existing government departments. There was a definite purpose in the Belgian mind when this approach was planned. They had already learned, during the war, that the introduction of too many Europeans was in itself a potential danger to their own régime. Although the Congo was in urgent and pressing need of skilled technicians, the Belgians were quite determined that, so far as possible, they should be trained amongst local Congolese. In this respect, the Belgians are entitled to considerable kudos, even though their motives were founded on their determination to maintain the colonial *status quo*. It was, of course, necessary to introduce Belgian technicians for specialised research projects. Such personnel were carefully selected, and were used, in many instances, to train the Africans.

It was this determination to create native technicians, coupled with the technical aptitude shown by the Congolese themselves, that dulled not merely the suspicions of the United States, ever watchful against colonial aspirations, but, indeed, those of non-Western states. The Congo came to be looked upon as the ideal colony—a colony which was constantly used as a whip to lash the other colonial powers who could neither show commensurate native standards of living, nor technical skills of equal quality to those of the Congolese. It is doubtful if the general ignorance of colonial affairs on the part of those who ought to have known better was ever so clearly demonstrated; nor were so many alleged authorities on colonial matters ever so completely fooled.

Chapter Eight

STEMMING THE TIDE

DESPITE the Belgian haste to repair the damage to their policy of cultural isolation in the Congo, there were certain matters over which they had little control. There was, and always will be, in Africa a nomadic section of the population which can never be regulated. It was this native element which did so much to spread the gospel of independence in the areas south of the Sahara and which, by its very nature, was as uncontrollable as it was effective.

The independence of India in the immediate post-war years was the first big step forward in the march of colonial peoples towards freedom. There is a large Indian population in east and south Africa, and the general rejoicing with which they hailed the freeing of their homeland soon found a response in many African hearts. With the African's remarkable ability for transmitting good news over vast areas of bush, the people of the Congo (although most of them knew practically nothing about India) were soon made aware of this event.

India was only the beginning. Political consciousness in Africa quickly grew into a living force. Nigeria, although one of the most recent territories to achieve independence, took the lead. This was due to Herbert Macauley and Nnamdi Azikiwe who organised the National Council for Nigeria and the Cameroons. Azikiwe, or 'Zik' as he was commonly known, had lived in America and had learned much of American politics and politicians. This, added to his own outstanding ability and genuine love of Africa, made him a formidable political figure. It is not an exagger-

ation to say that no other single individual on the west
coast of Africa has done more to awaken political consciousness in the British, French and Belgian West African
colonies than Zik. The news of his mission on behalf of the
National Council for Nigeria and the Cameroons, amply
publicised through the newspapers he had established in
Nigeria, spread rapidly, not only in the British territories,
but also in the French. The constant stream of unofficial
travellers between the French Congo and the Belgian
colony soon carried his word and ideology throughout the
length and breadth of the country. His claim that all
Africans had a right to independence and self-determination was a sweet sound even to the illiterate masses so
assiduously insulated against outside influence by the
Belgians.

The riots in Ghana, which were the prelude to its independence, also made news in the most remote areas in
Africa south of the Sahara. The idea began to filter through,
slowly at first, that violence for political reasons was the
barometer of dissatisfaction in the colonies; that it excited
sympathy abroad, particularly in America, and that it was
also a clear indication of the African resentment of the
domination of white over black.

The Belgian attitude to all this was a strange mixture of
toleration and patronising self-satisfaction. They believed
that they possessed an effective antidote to what they regarded as the antics of power-drunk rabble-rousers :
raising living standards to a degree unknown amongst
African labourers in any other part of the continent;
limited concessions in education; and, in general, the creation for the African of an environment which, while
providing considerable bodily comfort, would foster mental
lethargy. On one aspect of policy the Belgians were determined : there was to be no encouragement of the strivings
towards political responsibility; nor was there to be any
change of attitude which would suggest ultimate independence for the Congolese. Guy Mallengreau in his speech at

Washington in 1954 summed up the Belgian doctrine admirably when he said : 'Belgians are a people of common sense, a profoundly realistic nation, whose constant guide is a cautious empiricism. If their colonial policy does not display evidences of boundless imagination or excessive boldness, its results do show stable and constant progress. Belgians have no colonial doctrine as such, for their faithful attachment to reality rules out preconceived notions. Neither the war nor the largely unjust criticisms of some international organizations has persuaded the Belgians to throw over their policy of common sense and prudence in favour of rash and apparently generous reforms from which the natives ultimately will be the first to suffer.'

Paternalism was steadily developed as a barrier to the growing sense of Congolese nationalism. The Belgians never attempted to answer the charge that the Congolese African, in spite of his advanced material environment, was kept at a lower human level than the whites. They denied strongly that any racial bias existed, maintaining that their relationship to the Congolese was simply that of father to son. In one of their official publications entitled *The Belgian Congo* (*Forty Questions and Answers*), which was widely distributed outside Belgium, the following paragraph is to be found : 'The Congo does not recognise segregation. In reality, a great effort must be made in every field to overcome the tendency of both racial groups to live amongst themselves. In order to combat this segregation at the start, the Government has adopted measures for facilitating native children's admittance into European schools, and no mention is ever made of the parents' standing. The teachers are required to give particular attention to the mutual conduct of European and Congolese children.'

They did admit, however, of a legislative discrimination between natives and non-natives and of a social barrier between the natives themselves. The latter was a deliberate creation and was closely tied to the post-war education system in the Congo, which is dealt with in the following chapter. The idea was nothing new in colonial policy, although the Belgians were trying it out in an original environment. They had destroyed the power of the chiefs, the traditional leaders who would be the natural recipients of social prestige, and transferred it to personnel of their own choice.

The method employed to achieve this social badge of their paternalistic benevolence was the creation of the civic merit card. This was granted to Africans who were not polygamous, who had never been guilty of any serious crimes, who were over twenty-one and who were able to read, write and do simple mathematical calculations. There was one overall requirement which stated that a man had to give evidence of good conduct and habits as a proof of his genuine desire to participate in the further quest of civilisation. It is evident that these conditions allow of almost maximum elasticity in interpretation, and when one considers that at the granting of independence there were less than two thousand card holders, it will be appreciated how effectively to their own advantage the conditions were interpreted by the Belgians. Incidentally, one of the somewhat strange privileges attached to the merit card was that a holder could not be flogged if he did not turn out to be all that was expected.

Because of the carefully conceived plan to maintain the Congolese in this *status quo* in the face of the political murmurings on all sides, the Belgian Congo was still something of a colonial showpiece in the eyes of the Western world. To what extent relative sincerity and just plain ignorance of the facts contributed to this thinking is hard to tell. One very interesting embellishment of the American attitude may throw some light on the matter. It was remembered that the Belgians, living in a small, defenceless country, had been the victims of two world wars and had twice been overrun, occupied and brutally subjugated by the Germans. How could such a long-suffering nation, with

such vivid personal memories, seriously ill-treat their own
African subjects? For far too long the Americans believed
that such treatment was virtually the private hallmark of
British imperialism, a belief strengthened by the fact that
the American people are so often swayed, particularly in
their political life, by emotion. The contrast between the
powerful British Empire and the tiny kingdom of Belgium
was too strong for commonsense.

Why did the liberal-minded section of the Belgian public
not interest itself in the Congo natives' predicament? This
question, often asked, is easily answered. The Congolese
student did all his studies (if they could be so called) at
home in the Congo; interchange of students between the
two countries was an entirely reprehensible idea to the
authorities, while education on colonial affairs in Belgium
was such that it presented a picture of profound gratitude
and content on the part of the native. From the colonial
territories of other powers, many hundreds of students
travelled abroad and made contact with other peoples. The
resurgence of interest in Africa after the Second World War
was such that these Africans received something akin to
favoured nation treatment in schools, colleges and in industrial organisations. Many of them turned 'professional'
Africans and became expert in the technique of exciting
sympathy, especially, in the United States. A few years
ago it was almost impossible to complain to an American
that one of the most ill-informed people in the world about
his own country was the African student. In the great
majority of instances, his background, prior to going abroad
to pursue his studies, had been the narrow environment
of an isolated town or village, from which he never moved
until he left home to begin his studies.

In the case of the Congo there were no students travelling
abroad to disseminate information, either true or false,
about it. There were no business trainees either, nor, in
fact, was there created abroad any atmosphere likely to
turn attention to the Congo and foster political interest in

it, as had been the case for instance, with Kenya, Nigeria and Ghana.

Despite the fact that the standards of living of the Congolese had been raised very considerably, there was one aspect of the economy which militated against their having business contact with those outside the colony. This was all the more interesting because of its complete divergence from the current practice in the British territories. In the latter, in order to cushion the African producer of cash crops, like cocoa, palm produce, cotton and groundnuts, against world markets, Produce Marketing Boards* were established in all the British West African colonies. One of the first tasks of these boards was to use every media possible to instruct the farmers in the bush about their functions, the methods of finance and the inevitable price fluctuations in world markets. No effort was made to conceal any of the important factors governing such an operation. Added to this, the boards financed frequent journeys to Europe and America by young produce inspectors, farmers' leaders and other personnel for the purpose of seeing at first hand the manufacture and ultimate use of their produce.

The Belgian approach was entirely different. They built up a strong internal market to an extent that lessened the effects of a sudden fluctuation in external demand. The anticipated long-term result of this was the assurance of real prosperity for artisan and peasant alike. The really important aspect of it was an unspoken one : it kept the African at home; it avoided the situation in which he could have serious economic contact with the outside world; and it engendered the idea that the happy combination of Belgian and Congolese was above the mundane trafficking in the world outside.

And so for twelve years after the war the Belgian Congo

* The author was the first Public Relations officer for the four Nigerian Marketing Boards, to which post he was appointed in 1951.

with its beautiful façade of prosperity and contentment fooled the world, just as did Leopold II. Did it fool the Belgians, or were they so enamoured of their own achievement that they failed to realise that this impression was so very like Africa itself—calm, green and peaceful to the watcher from a distance, but wild and explosive within?

CHAPTER NINE

CATHOLICISM AND EDUCATION

FROM the early days of Leopold's régime, Catholicism has been the predominant influence in Congolese education (such as it is). The Papal Decree of Leo XIII enabled nuns and priests, who were also teachers, to be treated as civil servants and to be paid accordingly. Many of them were members of religious orders which demanded vows of poverty so that their accumulated salaries went into institutional funds thus ensuring that the financial struggles experienced by Catholic missionaries in other African territories had no place in the Congo. The Jesuit order (The Belgian Society of Jesus)—that intellectual bulwark of militant Catholicism—was one of the congregations active in Congolese education.

Although the Protestant missionaries were the very first to go to the Congo during the Leopold régime, for reasons already explained in a previous chapter, in a short time they took second place to Catholicism. So strong was the influence of the latter that it was only during the last few years that missionaries, other than Catholic, received any real encouragement and any financial assistance.

From Leopold's time and until 1950, primary education marked the highest level of academic achievement in the Congo. Most of that time the Catholic Church, as well as having the greatest influence, was the educative authority making annual reports to the Belgian Government. It laid down the required standards and was fully aware of the restrictive nature of the academic training given to the Congolese.

65

How was this imposition compatible with Catholic teaching? Theologians have nearly always agreed that Rome advanced with the *Summa Theologica* of St. Thomas Aquinas in one hand and The Bible in the other. The *Summa* clearly defines patriotism as a virtue; yet in the Congo, the Catholic teachers lent themselves to an educational policy which was geared specifically to the task of suppressing the kind of education out of which patriotism grows. It has been avowed very truthfully that the Catholic missionaries in the Congo were Belgians first and Catholics afterwards.

The answer offered by Catholic moral theologians to this charge is that their education was in accordance with the laws of the State and their main function was the spiritual destiny of the Congolese natives. They argued that the very sparse academic education they provided was sufficient to enable the Congolese to reach the required spiritual level. This answer is entirely unsatisfactory and contrary to Thomistic teaching. Even if the fact that patriotism is a virtue is disregarded, Aquinas also clarifies in the *Summa* the essence of law when he says 'since every part is ordained to the whole as the imperfect to the perfect and since one man is a part of the perfect community, law must needs concern itself properly with the order directed to universal happiness'. In the same treatise he stated that law is 'referable to the common good, not as to a common genus or species'.*

At one and the same time the Catholic missionaries were civil servants and spiritual leaders. By the very nature of their calling, their primary duty was to the spiritual destiny of man, and according to Catholic theology, patriotism is one of the virtues which contributes to this destiny. It would appear, therefore, that when their dual function militated against the spiritual they should have abandoned civil service status and have accepted for themselves spiritual freedom. The latter is an absolute requisite of many

* Question 90, Article 3 of the *Summa*.

thousands of Catholic missionaries working in numerous other colonial areas. Such freedom would have allowed honest application to the kind of education compatible with Catholic belief.

The Catholic Church in the Congo must have realised that its narrow attitude was bound to lead to a most unfavourable comparison with the Church's work in other African areas. The Maryknoll missionaries in the United States, in a journal called *World Campus*, which has a very wide circulation in most American colleges and universities, in an article published in March, 1960, made the following statement : 'Catholicism is the very backbone of African intellectualism—on which Africa must draw to control her rapidly developing freedom. Even in South Africa, where every single obstacle is placed in the way of decent education for Africans, the Catholic Church managed to establish outside Durban in Natal a college for training African teachers. It is the famous Mariannhill Mission which started as a Cistercian monastery, founded by German monks. The conditions of living were such, and the need for education so urgent, that some forty years ago the Vatican agreed to the monastery becoming a special missionary society known as the Marriannhill Mission. Wherever in the Union of South Africa there are facilities for education, there will be found teachers from Mariannhill. It was a student from this school—afterwards a Catholic priest—who became the first African to be appointed to a professorship in a South African university. The work of the White Fathers in East Africa needs little introduction. If it were possible to investigate the individual careers of the many young men who are rallying around Mboya, Nyerere and Banda, it would be realised quickly that in many an African heart, love of country—which has produced the wave of nationalism throughout the continent—sprang from Catholic teaching and from the knowledge that patriotism is a Christian virtue. No other missionary church in Africa teaches this as an actual doctrine.'

Even such comparisons left the Congolese missionary educators unmoved. It did, however, answer the question why there were no American Catholic missionaries in the Congo. The Belgian Catholic hierarchy is reputed, on good authority, to have made it abundantly clear to the various Catholic organisations in the United States that they would not be welcome in the Belgian Congo. The reason is obvious; they were afraid that American missionaries would propagate nationalistic ideas which would not be in keeping with Belgian policy. So careful was Catholicism in preserving the *status quo* in the Congo that they sent a priest to the United States to act as troubleshooter. His specific task was to answer difficult questions pertaining to Belgian education in the Colony. Another priest who was sent to the United Nations lobbied very successfully in a similar manner in the delegates' lounges.

The suppression and limitation of education in the Congo, and particularly in Ruanda Urundi, did not go unchallenged. The Commission on Trust Territories at the United Nations Assembly in 1952 condemned the Belgian educational restrictions and demanded that in the trusteeship territory, Ruanda Urundi, over which the United Nations had authority, greater facilities for secondary and higher education should be offered. The effect of this interference was to cause a limited reorganisation in Belgian educational policy, but the improvements made still left the system too restricted for any steps to be taken that might have avoided the present situation.

The primary education system of the Belgians, and the technical training which accompanied it, created in the Congo a lower middle class, but no professional class which could have taken over the reins of government in a crisis. The limits to which this was carried can best be judged from the almost unbelievable fact that, at the present moment, there is not a single trained Congolese lawyer. This probably is more condemnatory of the Belgian ideology than most of its other crimes of omission.

In every other single African territory where political consciousness has helped the drive towards independence, native lawyers have been in the forefront, just as they were in the days of the French Revolution. The Belgian Government was obviously fully aware that the legal profession presented a danger and for that reason, took no steps that might lead to Congolese lawyers working with either whites or blacks.

The Belgians had worked out a special training system, with the aid of Catholic professors, which was set in operation in 1948 and which lasted until 1954. It called for two distinct organisations. One was known as FOMULAC (a name derived from the Belgian sponsors of the organisation), which was established at Kisantu to train male nurses and medical assistants. The second one, named CADULAC, established in the same place, gave elementary education in agriculture. In 1957, also at Kisantu, a third group was set up and was called the School of General Administration.

The Jesuits had these three organisations under their direct control. How they could have justified their determination to prevent any of the students attending these institutions from advancing to full professional qualification, is difficult of comprehension. There is one other factor worthy of mention. For fifty years no attempt was made to educate Congolese women. The only move in this direction was a very recent decision. It was not until 1954, when pressure was brought to bear in the United Nations (and then, only after much resistance on the part of the Belgians), that a proper university was established.

Yet, despite all this, the Belgians still prided themselves on their making the Congo the only country in Africa that could show fifty per cent of the children of school age attending school. Of this fifty per cent, they claimed that seventy per cent were boys. It is perfectly true that, on a *pro rata* basis, the Belgians did have the largest number of Africans attending school, and it was this statistic that blinded the rest of the world to the quality of the education

provided. Had the Belgians had any genuine desire to train
their people, they had the organisations available. In the
Jesuits, they had men of very great intellectual stature who
were members of one of the finest teaching bodies in the
world. It is little wonder that Catholicism is being criticised
so severely for its action in the Congo.

The Belgians attempted to fill the gap created by the
absence of secondary education by devoting particular
attention to the entertainment of their young people. Side
by side with this, they conducted a campaign of mass
education—a technique which has become very popular
and which has been copied and improved upon by various
other organisations. One of the media they adopted was an
enormous film programme, which is probably the best of its
kind in Africa. This also was organised by Catholic missionaries and became known as the 'Congo Catholic Cinema
Centre'. It acted as a religious-cum-social supplement to
government propaganda and produced well over a hundred
original films for mass education.

In Leopoldville, a huge stadium was built—a vast concrete structure capable of seating seventy-five thousand
spectators. This was another of the amenities which the
missionaries produced as a means of providing recreation
for the leisure hours of the Congolese. They also set up
Christian working youth organisations and, in fact, produced a general level of welfare which caused Mr. Jean L.
Comhaire, now one of the leading social study authorities
in the United States, to say : 'Leopoldville, thanks to the
generous help given by the Government to the missions, has
a more comprehensive system of social welfare than obtains
anywhere else in Africa.'

Welfare was a poor substitute for the intellectual craving
which was lying dormant in the African. The policy of the
Belgians was clear cut and was voiced to John J. Considine,
author of *Africa, World of New Men*, by Father Van Wing,
S.J., Secretary of the Committee of Mission Superiors, and
doyen of the pioneers of Catholic policy in public life in the

Congo. The Jesuit summed it up as follows when he stated
that the inalienable rights of workers were (1) a just salary;
(2) a family salary; (3) humane working conditions; (4) a
decent habitation for the family.

There was no mention whatever of those rights which
spring from a truly democratic system—no reference whatever to any political idea of self-determination. In the event
that this left anyone in doubt, Governor General Leo
Petillon of the Belgian Congo, in an official speech in 1953,
subsequent to the United Nations' intervention in regard
to education, declared that the United Nations' desire for
speed was ill-advised. He said : 'We know these tendencies.
They are inspired by ideologies that, at first glance, seem
generous, but are utopian. They are built on impatience,
they are calculated to incite us to do things, no matter how,
in impatient haste. They are calculated to lead us to ignore
the lessons of long experience, dearly acquired, for reasons
of political opportunism.'

When the University of Louvain was established in 1954
at Kimuenza, fifteen miles outside Leopoldville, the Belgians made much of the idea of creating a new *élite* in the
Congo. In the first place, the university was a concession
forced on them by circumstances. But still they made no
reference to the creation of an upper middle class which
would act as the backbone of a sound, healthy political
movement. Rather they referred constantly to the fact that
slowness was to be the keynote of the new venture. In point
of fact, only a very few Congolese qualified for entry to the
university and although it had been planned years earlier,
most of those who succeeded were still forced to take one
or two years of pre-university study. Four courses were
offered—medicine, leading to a full doctorate; a university
degree in agriculture; a university degree in administration;
and a university degree in education. Even at this late
stage, there was no suggestion that the Congolese were to
have the opportunity to study law—an absolute essential in

any young country where there was any intention of establishing racial equality or equality of opportunity.

At this time, in Britain, in America (and unfortunately,
behind the Iron Curtain), there were hundreds of students
studying in foreign universities. Figures for students studying in the United States' institutions of higher education are
available for 1956. They show that while there were 226
from Nigeria, there were only three from the Congo. This
extraordinary disparity is startling and is in itself a serious
and apparently indefensible indictment of both Belgian and
Catholic educative aspirations in the Congo.

Chapter Ten

THE DEATH OF PATERNALISM

BELGIAN paternalism perished ingloriously on 4th January, 1959. Sentence of death was not promulgated by any written document. It was written in blood on the streets of Leopoldville. On that day the Belgian Government banned a meeting of the Association of the Lower Congo, commonly known as the Abako. As a result of the ban, rioting broke out in Leopoldville and lasted two whole days. According to the official Belgian report, about fifty persons were killed while 300 were injured. It is most probable that the casualty figures were many times higher. The lack of accurate information about the rioting marked the beginning of an era of confusion and obscurity which still overshadows truth.

Never in the history of colonialism has any nation been so stunned as were the Belgians during these days. The blow was as shattering as it was sudden, although realisation of its significance came quickly enough. The walls of the Belgian cultural compound came crashing down, and out of what the Belgians had believed to be the comfort and contentment of the Congolese arose that terrifying colonial monster, 'Independence'. The Leopoldville riots were only the beginning; many others followed.

Why was the collapse of paternalism so sudden? This is a question that has been asked time and again. The real question, however, is: Was it so sudden? The answer appears to be that it was not, but that the Belgians, both at home and in the Congo, had become so enamoured of their own achievement that they failed to realise what was going on around them. Between the years 1945 and 1960, contact between the Belgian authorities and the Congolese people never returned to its pre-World War II status. The Belgians were apparently unaware of this, although there were a few Africans in the Congo who were beginning to exploit it. There was ample evidence that the rot had set in.

The development of the Abako itself was one of the first indications that an anti-colonial movement was in being. The organisation had been founded in 1955 with a purely cultural purpose under the leadership of Joseph Kasavubu who was a clerk in the Finance Department of the Colonial Government. Gradually, it developed into a political movement, particularly after 1958. Kasavubu, like most leaders in the Congo, had been taught in a Catholic mission school and at one time was an aspirant to the priesthood. This was one of the many routes by which some of Africa's better known native politicians began their journeys to national leadership. Another party, which was formed a year later, was the Congolese National Movement under the leadership of Patrice Lumumba. Strangely enough both these parties had the blessing of the Belgian Government and their political leanings were, in fact, encouraged by Maurice van Hemelrijck. The latter was the first Belgian colonial minister to believe that nationalism—a nationalism which could be controlled and gradualised by the Belgians —was a possibility. He had succeeded, as Governor General of the Congo, Leon Petillon who refused to countenance any thought of self-government for the Congolese, although on occasion he is reputed to have paid lip service to it as an ideal for the very distant future. Hemelrijck had been influenced, as indeed had a number of Belgians and Congolese, by an article written in 1955 by a Belgian newspaperman, Joseph van Bilsen, who was teaching at the Institute for Colonial Studies in Antwerp and who had put forward a proposal which seemed extremely radical to most Belgians : that a plan should be worked out for the grant of independence to the Congo in thirty years. In his article he said : 'If we have no plan worthy of confidence, we will encounter tensions and irrepressible movements.' Because of its radical nature and because it planted the idea of self-government in the minds of a number of literate Congolese, this article, as well as the proposals it contained, received considerable publicity in the Congo itself. When Hemelrijck took over from Petillon, whose policy has been described as that of 'paternal gradualism', he realised that political feeling had to be considered as a factor in the Belgian Congo. This feeling, incidentally, was not nationalism in the sense that we know it; it was much more an expression of anti-colonialism. Whatever its precise nature, it failed to stir any sense of real apprehension in the minds of the Belgians.

Again, since 1955, the bush telegraph had become more active than ever; Ghana had become independent; Nigeria was about to realise its freedom; and General de Gaulle had made his famous speech of August 24th, 1959, in which he stated : 'Whoever desires independence can immediately obtain it.' The independence of French colonial territories is stale history, but its immediate effect on the Congolese has never yet been fully recorded.

It was only natural, with all this political activity going on, and the wonderful source of news it provided for the African nomads, that the urge to control its own destiny should have been born and nurtured in the Congo at this period.

If any proof were needed that the majority of Belgians were either deliberately blinding themselves to what was going on or were intentionally trying to frustrate all aspirations towards freedom, they were well aware that Minister Hemelrijck had been heckled and had been the recipient of rotten eggs and tomatoes hurled at him by Belgian workers in the Congo. In fact, he had earned for himself the nick-name of *Momo la Terreur*, a nickname which was supposed to indicate that he was recklessly encouraging political advancement in the Congo. Despite his unpopularity, and in face of opposition from the Belgians, in December 1958 he did permit Lumumba and two colleagues to attend the All-African Peoples Conference in Accra. An interesting aspect of all this was that Kasavubu was not permitted to make the journey. The latter, however, consoled himself with injecting new political vigour into the Abako—to such good effect that it exploded in January 1959.

The Belgians recovered quickly from this shattering blow, believing, with typical Belgian aplomb, that they could handle the changing situation just as successfully as they had dealt with events after World War II. Unhappily they failed to realise that this time they were faced with a genuine and quite uncontrollable hatred on the part of the Africans. However, within ten days of the Leopoldville riots, they proposed a programme for the gradual attainment of self-rule. Later in the year, on October 16th, Monsieur Auguste de Schrijver called for the election by adult male suffrage of rural and municipal councils.

Van Hemelrijck had resigned in disgust some months earlier because he realised that the Belgians still clung too closely to the idea of gradualism. Immediately after the January riots Kasavubu had been put in prison for inciting to riot—an incident which is wrapped in some considerable mystery. Hemelrijck released him after a couple of months and arranged to have him taken to Brussels secretly. What went on in Brussels is not fully known, but it appears that Kasavubu had, at that time, ideas of Balkanising the Congo and establishing the Republic of Central Congo in Leopoldville Province alone.

In addition to the elections for the councils, the Belgians promised that in 1960 two parliamentary chambers would be set up in the Congo and that they would be granted considerable, but by no means complete, power. They also undertook that, after four years, the proposed new régime would be examined in order that future relationships might be established. They hoped that this would provide them with five years of grace to examine the problem thoroughly and make plans for their future position in the colony.

It is clear that they hoped that they could establish the kind of constitutional machinery that had worked so successfully in Ghana and Nigeria. They had seen that little violence in either of these territories had preceded independence; in fact, the only serious riots in Nigeria had occurred between the Nigerians themselves. The Belgians, as a people, have a horror of violence and it is to their credit that a very honest desire to avoid bloodshed was a predominant factor during these most crucial days.

The Belgian hope to establish a pattern similar to that of the British territories, as well as their plan for speedy gradualism, was unlikely to succeed. They did not realise the degree to which an impasse was threatening, or that the African leaders had learned something about the delaying tactics of colonial powers as well as some embarrassing political techniques of their own. Kasavubu, who had returned to his own country, decided to boycott the proposed elections, while Lumumba, in the areas where Kasavubu was not influential, obtained eighty per cent of the votes. This was the immediate signal for further pressure on the part of the Congolese leaders.

At this point it is important to study the main factors motivating in the African leaders. Was it true nationalism as we know it? Neither Kasavubu nor Lumumba had the real educational background or experience to appreciate how nationalism could be nurtured and fostered. Lumumba had been sent to prison in 1957 for embezzlement and was very much of an opportunist. He did, however, have his prison experience as a badge of merit—once described as an 'absolute *sine qua non* for a good African politician'. Kasavubu (and subsequent events prove this) enjoyed a certain understanding of ideology, but he lacked, and still does, the power to control people and inspire them. One important factor stands out : neither of these leaders appreciated that the qualities which they brought to their tasks could possibly be compared with those of the African leaders in the nearby British and French territories. There is little evidence even now that they have learned how great is this difference.

Although Nigerians originally demanded independence as early as 1956—and could have had it then—they later agreed that it would be much wiser to have a waiting period of four years. Neither Lumumba nor Kasavubu ever gave evidence of having the wisdom, the true patriotism, to consider delay as a possibility. The pride of the African is one of his most outstanding qualities—at times endearing, often infuriating. Because of the hundreds of years in which he has had to live in a position of inequality, the idea of even remotely backing down is far harder for him to accept than it is for the average European. This is one of the psychological factors which have caused so much chaos in the Congo, for most of the Congolese leaders have lost themselves in prideful attachment to their own importance.

The next move in the Congolese advance was a meeting, held at Kisantu between December 24th and 27th, 1959, of a number of African organisations. These, for want of better terminology, might be called emergent national parties, and included such bodies as the Katanga Baluba Association, the Progressist Rural Alliance, the African Association of the Upper Congo Peoples, the Mongo Union and a number of others. When the Round Table Conference took place in Brussels early in 1960, there were altogether some twenty-one Congolese associations represented. Only a few of these, however, were present at the Kisantu Conference because at that time they were not sufficiently well organised; nor, for that matter, were they fully aware of what was going on. The meeting passed a resolution to the effect that independence should be granted at once.

This second blow did not by any means affect the Belgians like the initial one, but they still endeavoured to slow down the Africans in a manner which would enable them to reorganise their ideas. They failed completely.

As a result of this failure, the Belgians realised suddenly —very suddenly—that there was little purpose in putting further effort into the job of holding on. It was now their turn to administer a shock. With what looked like a gesture of almost complete abandonment, they called a Round Table Conference in Brussels (which is dealt with in the next chaper) in mid-January, 1960, and there agreed to grant full independence to the Congolese in the following June.

At the time the Belgians made this decision, they were fully aware that there was not a single capable Congolese administrator in the whole colony. Why did they do it? No one has yet answered this question satisfactorily, other than to put forward the theory that it suggested the behaviour of a sulky child. They expressed bitterness and disappointment because Britain and France did not support them; because the United Nations and the United States were exerting pressure on them. All the same, they could have appealed to the United Nations to act as an interim authority before relinquishing their hold on the colony. This would probably have prevented the present chaos.

On the other hand it would be unfair to put all the blame on the Belgians; the United Nations must accept some of the responsibility as, indeed, must the other colonial powers. Their long experience in Africa with the childish mentality of the uneducated African should have warned them of what was likely to happen.

The Belgians themselves have never openly accepted the blame, but they were fully aware that there were only 247 students at Louvanium University and not a single full graduate among them; that there were only seventeen university students in Ruanda Urundi; that there were fewer than 25,000 Africans in the whole of the Belgian Congo who had received any kind of secondary training at all.

It has been suggested that the Belgians had simply

accepted the inevitable, still hoping that they could establish after independence some kind of arrangement similar to the British Commonwealth whereby they and the Congolese would be able to work together to their mutual benefit. This is a credible reason for their sudden change of heart, for after all it was common knowledge that the British African territories had agreed to enter the Commonwealth. On the other hand, they must also have realised that they had already created the very barrier which would prevent any such co-operation. This was the limitation of Congolese education. How could they ever really have hoped that an atmosphere of mutual trust could be created between a people so ill-equipped in self-government and their former masters who had been forced to abdicate through their own stupidity? On the other hand, it may be that, even at this late stage, the Belgians still believed in their old philosophy—that fuller stomachs, better houses and bigger circuses would offset any reaction to the injustices of the past.

CHAPTER ELEVEN

INDEPENDENCE AND INSINCERITY

SEVENTY-FOUR years, almost to the day, after the conclusion of the Berlin Conference, the Belgo-Congolese Round Table Conference assembled in Brussels in mid-January 1960. Each of these conferences had a profound effect on the fate of the Congo. The first one condemned the territory to a long period of Belgian colonialism, the second to immature independence. The Belgian reigning monarch was present on each occasion; numerous high-flown speeches concluded each gathering; and each brought down tragedy and suffering on the heads of the unfortunate Congolese.

Kasavubu and Lumumba were among the many African delegates at the Round Table Conference, as was Tshombe from Katanga. Kasavubu caused the meeting to get off to a bad start. Although the conference assembled only in the middle of January, he demanded independence by March 1st, 1960. On being informed that the Belgians would not consider such a demand, he walked out and did not return to the meeting. Carrying on without him, Lumumba then demanded June 1st as independence day; the Belgians countered with August 1st and after considerable squabbling, and with something suggestive of a gesture of abandonment, they compromised on June 30th.

The date having been agreed, the conference met on February 20th to hear the numerous final speeches from the Africans and the Belgians. King Baudouin delivered a special speech to the delegates on February 21st, 1960.

In the light of subsequent events, these speeches are interesting, for if ever proof were needed to show that oratory is the harlot of the arts, it was to be found there. The only remarks compatible with the insincerity of the occasion were the numerous references to the great work of Leopold II.

Departing from chronological order, the royal speech provides as good a starting point as any to study the spoken words at a conference which proved completely ineffective, utterly insincere and, as far as one can see at the present, a waste of time. King Baudouin said : 'More than ever our thoughts turn to Leopold II, who founded the Congo State some eighty years ago. From a completely unexplored wilderness, unknown to most of the world, from a variety of races and tribes mainly hostile to each other and victims of the slave trade and disease, a mighty empire has grown.'

One cannot but ask, where is the might? Where is the empire?

Although the monarch's speech concluded the Round Table Conference and was, in effect, no more than a courtesy, it did mark colonial defeat in Belgium and a new triumph for Africa on the march. The really important speeches were made by Lumumba and Tshombe. One can only regret that Mr. Kasavubu did not make an oratorical contribution to the occasion. It would have been interesting to compare, in the light of the Congo today, his views with those of his erstwhile colleagues.

In previous chapters no reference has been made to Mr. Moise Tshombe who entered the political picture for the first time at the Brussels Conference. Tshombe, a successful Katanga businessman, came to the conference as President of the Confederation of Katanga Associations, an organisation which had hitherto been completely ineffective. Tshombe was obviously one of the shrewdest of the delegates and his speech at the conference gives us a clear-cut idea of both the man and his purpose. The following is an excerpt : 'We greatly hope that between now and June 30th, and after the Congo's accession to independence, law, order and peace will prevail in the Congo. We shall do everything in our power to ensure it. We are fully conscious of the risk that the independent Congo may lose the benefit of the social and economic progress bestowed on it by Belgium, and may even fall behind unless it continues to benefit from Belgian financial and technical assistance, and also unless new capital investments are forthcoming.

'It is therefore with joy that we have taken note of the unanimous engagement contracted by the Congolese delegations to apply the principles of the Declaration of the Rights of Man in the Congo, to respect persons, property and investments, and to seek for bases of agreements which will notably include the treaties to be freely and independently signed with Belgium.'

From the beginning, Lumumba was the real firebrand; he came to the Conference as President of the Congolese National Movement and, since Kasavubu had left, was the strongest African leader there. In his speech he was definite about the maintenance of the friendliest relations with the Belgians, although he was quite decisive in expressing his objectives for the Congo of the future. Referring to future Congolese-Belgian relations he summarised the Congolese objectives as follows :

1. The creation, in all parts of the Congo, of an atmosphere of confidence and calm so that the new institutions may be set up in a spirit of joy and fraternal co-operation.

2. The eradication of every vestige of colonialism, notably by the immediate elimination of every trace of racial discrimination and the unjust laws passed under the colonial régime.

3. The immediate cessation of the oppressive measures currently being taken against the local population in some regions of the Congo.

4. The consolidation of national independence by the creation of a stable and prosperous national economy. Our independence will have no significance unless it contributes to the improvement of living standards of the worker and peasant classes.

As well as laying down the goals the Congolese had in view, Lumumba made one interesting statement which is worthy of mention. He said : 'Capital investment in the Congo will be respected, for we are an honest people. As for the Belgian civil servants now working in the Congo, we would ask them to serve our government with the same loyalty as they served the Belgian Government. They may all be proud of their humanitarian contribution to a work of national reconstruction. A young state, we shall need the advice and technical assistance of Belgium. We sincerely hope that this assistance will not be refused. We would appeal fraternally to the democratic youth of Belgium to come and serve the Congolese state. Here you will find a brotherly nation in need of other brothers. As for the tribal chieftains, we would ask them to acknowledge the need for evolution and to co-operate with the political leaders in building their country. We shall reserve them an honour-able place in our future institutions. Citizens of the Congo, we ask you to unite and combine your efforts so as to build a great, united, strong, hardworking and prosperous nation in the heart of Central Africa.'

Lumumba's speech, as well as many of his subsequent actions, point to a complete disregard for sincerity or reliability. A week after the declaration of the Congo's in-dependence, he began a campaign which was aimed directly at complete severance from Belgium. His behaviour at the Round Table Conference can only be attributed to a desire to clear the way for well-prepared plans (these are dealt with in the following chapter) which were to include the Communists and not the Western powers.

There were also speeches by Belgian ministers; the most significant of these was that made by the Belgian Prime Minister, Mr. Gaston Eyskens, who, amongst other things, made some statements which must always stand as a serious indictment of the Belgian Government. The most damning was : 'We have no illusions concerning the immense work there is to do in the educational field; nor are we unaware

of the ardent desire shared by so many of your compatriots
to accede to all levels of education. We are also aware of
the limited sources involved.' At least he was honest enough
not to advance unacceptable excuses for the lack of education in the colony.

He, too, referred to future Congolese-Belgian relations.
He said : 'Today, I can once more tell you how fully
Belgium realises the great responsibility she will still bear
in regard to the Congo. Belgium must provide the Congo
with technical assistance. Under conditions which we have
defined together, we are leaving you the qualified personnel
of the magistrature, the administration, the medical and
health corps, and all other bodies devoted to the spiritual,
moral and social welfare, the economic development and
prosperity of your country.'

The Prime Minister's words could so easily have been
the prelude to a healthy understanding, at least between
the Belgians and the Congolese, even if genuine friendship
was impossible. If the conference delegates had had any
true appreciation of the basic elements of civilised social
progress, they would have regarded this Belgian ready-
made administrative machine as vital to their future, all
the more so as it would have been theirs to control. Instead
Lumumba deliberately wrecked it.

Despite the obvious insincerity of purpose of some of the
delegates, the Round Table Conference, on the practical
side, did outline the future constitutional pattern for the
Congo.

Altogether there were 254 articles specifying the complete and detailed system of government of the Congolese
state and the provinces. Central and provincial institutions
were to be established; the former were to comprise :

1. A chief of state.
2. A government at the head of which was to be
appointed a prime minister.
3. A house of representatives and a senate, together forming the parliament.

4. A judicial power, separate from the legislature and executive.

Also planned were economic and social councils and a constitutional court comprising three tribunals : one for constitutional affairs, one for disputes, and one for the administration.

The provincial institutions which were planned were :

1. A provincial government with a president at its head.
2. A provincial assembly.
3. A state commissioner representing the central power.

Section V of the proposed constitution specified the prerogatives of the central and provincial powers and enumerated their individual and exclusive responsibilities. Section VI stated the general terms concerning :

1. Civil servants.
2. The armed forces.
3. The announcement of official acts, as well as a few clauses relating to the transitional period.

Before closing on February 21st, the Round Table Conference agreed to the composition and duties of a second conference which met on April 26th and ended on May 16th. The purpose of this latter gathering was to plan the future economic, financial and social affairs of the Congo and to make orderly arrangements for the smooth transition of these affairs from the Belgians to the Congolese. Its tasks were enormous, for it had to wrestle with such problems as balancing the budget, the balance of payments, Belgian financial contributions to the Congo and a host of other economic nightmares. There was also the problem of Ruanda Urundi which was, as far as the Belgians were concerned, a part of the Congo but which, for the time being, would have to be administered separately by the Belgians, pending the decision of the United Nations.

The conference agreed that a joint committee to include delegates from Ruanda Urundi should be set up immediately following the conclusion of the conference. This committee was to be entrusted with the task of seeking a legal basis to ensure the continuance of the essential administrative machinery for taxation, customs and trade. It was decided that an agreement should be made between the Congo Government and the Government of Ruanda Urundi until the latter determined otherwise. On financial matters there was to be a special committee to study the forms of financial co-operation between the two countries.

Although this conference closed on May 16th, it was far from the completion of its task. In the first place, the parliamentary and provincial elections were to take place on the conclusion of the conference—a fact which provided a terrific incentive on the side of the Africans to end it. Also, the heady wine of freedom had taken hold of the Congolese delegates, acutely aware that the resources of their vast country were virtually in their grasp, and had forced on them an urgency that militated against rational behaviour.

There was, however, one very important aspect of the second conference which is deserving of recognition. It did succeed in making certain resolutions affecting some of the major social problems in the country. One of these resolutions is significant for it gives an indication of what was obviously going on in the minds of the Africans. It ran as follows:

The Conference,

1. notes that racial discrimination persists in the fundamental social laws enforced in the Congo, and that this discrimination should be eliminated without delay;
2. recommends that the Belgian Government shall amend these laws immediately by abolishing penal servitude for breaches of labour contracts and by aligning the regulations pertaining to mandatory

tillage with the 29th International Convention on
Forced Labour;

    3. recommends that the Congolese Government shall
replace the decrees on labour and employment contracts by a law regulating the engagement of all
Congolese workers irrespective of race or origin, and
the granting of legal status to collective agreements,
thus ensuring that all workers shall benefit from agreements concluded by their trade unions or professional
associations on their behalf;

    4. recommends that an agreement be concluded be-
tween the Congo and Belgium with the aim of guaran-
teeing to the employees and workers of both countries
free access to labour markets and the free transfer of
part of their emoluments.

As soon as the second conference finished, the stage—in
theory, if not in practice—was set for the Congo's entry
into self-government. As an interim measure, until the
elections were concluded, the Belgian Government decided
to send a resident minister to the Congo. He was Mr.
Ganshof van der Meersch, who was the Attorney General
of the Supreme Court of Appeals and was also Professor
of Law at the Université Libre de Bruxelles. His task was
to supervise the polling and ensure that disorders during
the election period would be controlled. For this purpose he
had instructions to strengthen the Force Publique.

Lumumba won the elections by a vast majority and was
promptly nominated as Premier by Van der Meersch.
Kasavubu became President of the new state. King
Baudouin made a congratulatory speech on June 30th.
The Belgian Congo had ceased to exist. Lumumba replied
to the Belgian Monarch's speech and immediately began to
show his true colours. His speech was churlish and aggre-
sive and he vented much of his spleen on Belgian colonialism. Lumumba had started to implement his own plans
for the Congo, and in doing so set up a process of disintegration that has not yet worked itself out.

CHAPTER TWELVE

LAND WITHOUT A LEADER

AT the Belgo-Congolese Round Table Conference every single speech, whether delivered by an African or a Belgian, concluded with two slogans : 'Long live the independent Congo' and 'Long live Belgium'. Patrice Lumumba added a third invokation when he added : 'Long live the friendship between our two peoples.' On the surface he appeared to be referring to relations between the Congolese and the Belgians, but what had he in mind, *really*? Did he *mean* the Belgians, or is it possible that his thoughts, sub-consciously if not consciously, were directed behind the Iron Curtain?

On July 1st, one of the first acts of Lumumba as Prime Minister was to address a cable to the Secretary-General of the United Nations requesting admission to membership of the body, in which he declared : 'That the Republic of the Congo accepts without reservation the obligations stipulated in the Charter of the United Nations and undertakes to abide by the same in absolute loyalty and good faith.'

On July 5th, the United Nations received from the Belgian Government a letter expressing its support for the admission of the Republic of the Congo to membership. On July 7th, the Security Council adopted resolutions recommending to the General Assembly that the Republic of the Congo be admitted to membership. This action virtually enjoined the Congo to act within the terms of the United Nations Charter.

Almost immediately following this, the Congolese Army mutinied. This was the prelude to an African nightmare which has brought the world to the edge of war, which has destroyed the economic structure of the Congo, and which has pushed the Congolese back into the arms of militant tribalism.

The causes of this mutiny are somewhat obscure. There must have been strong influences working on the army, for it is very doubtful that the eruption was spontaneous. The Congolese Army was a well-disciplined force; its living conditions were no worse than those of Ghanian and Nigerian troops, and, in fact, they were much better than what prevailed in many other African territories. If the Belgian discipline had been chafing too severely, why did the revolt not occur prior to independence? Why did the army have to wait until *after* independence when, supposedly, the cause of all injustices had been removed? The African soldier—that is, the fighting soldier—is amenable to discipline. His long tradition of taking orders and his knowledge of harsh tribal rule provide a background which he does not cast aside lightly. He is also, of course, a naïve person and very susceptible to influence. Consequently, there is a very considerable probability that the mutiny was largely the result of a prepared plan. The speed with which the Russians and the Czechs moved into the Congo immediately afterwards, the supplies of arms and ammunition which were almost immediately dispatched to the Congo, and particularly the urgency with which Lumumba demanded the immediate removal of all Belgians point to this fact.

In the light of subsequent events, it is obvious that all this was part of the Lumumba plan. As early as July 12th, the United Nations received a further cable demanding the urgent dispatch of United Nations military assistance. The reason given for this demand was that further Belgian troops were being sent to the Congo. This was so. But the reason for the dispatch of the Belgian troops was the unauthorised, unreasonable, and unprovoked attacks on Belgian civilians by the mutineering Congolese troops. The

United Nations dispatched its troops and promptly set up an organisation for rendering technical assistance to the Congolese. (See Appendix I.) The United Nations also demanded the immediate withdrawal of all Belgian troops from the Congo.

Up to this point, although by no means friendly, President Kasavubu and Lumumba were apparently working together. Then out of a blue sky came utter confusion. Kasavubu ousted Lumumba, Tshombe took over Katanga, and Mobutu, who had been appointed chief of staff immediately following the mutiny in the army, seized control of the government while Kasavubu and Lumumba were struggling for authority. Mobutu gave as his reasons for the coup that the quarrel of Kasavubu and Lumumba was causing constitutional disintegration. Mobutu lined up with Kasavubu. Mobutu had served for seven years in the ranks of the army and had left it to become a journalist. When the Congo had been granted independence he was appointed chief of staff. He was one of the few Congolese who had visited Belgium prior to the conferences marking independence. He had actually been sent there by the Catholic missionaries and while there attended courses at the Institute of Social Studies in Brussels.

To what extent the quarrel between Kasavubu and Lumumba can be attributed to the desire for personal power is difficult to say, although it might well have been that Kasavubu was aware that Lumumba, assisted by the Russians, was jockeying for a position of complete dictatorship. The United States Catholic and Welfare Council, which has at its disposal one of the most accurate news services in the country, released on August 22nd, a document which supports this. This document lists a series of secret instructions allegedly issued by Lumumba to the Bakusu tribe, which numbers some 200,000 members, during the June elections. The phraseology and content of the document are such that almost certainly it is of African origin. Excerpts from the text are as follows :

'Each Mukusu (singular of Bakusu) owes esteem and confidence to our liberator, Patrice Lumumba, the Congo's greatest leader.

'Never be afraid of convincing people of our superiority or of inspiring imitation of us, *for behind us we have a supreme power* that will help us in anything whatever, with no hesitation.

'After the other tribes are intimidated by our threats and shouting, we will be ready to submit them to our complete domination.

'Don't be afraid of spending money—we have plenty of it; this is the only tricky way to get the Congo into our hands easily. Without squandering money, we will not easily draw supporters, for the Congo must become our Anhutshu domain and possession.

'Don't forget that the white man is our enemy. Without him the Congo would already have been our domain, because during Arab times, our race had already ravaged several countries and had put them under our domination.

'The masses must be incited so that they never practice or believe the Christian religion, so that they can rebel against all missionaries and regular priests more easily.

'It is very necessary to send our own people to all the universities of the world—the largest number of them to Russia, where we will have the most privileges. The funds of our political leader, Lumumba, are for this especially.'

If the document is genuine it does offer a reasonable explanation for Lumumba's actions immediately following independence. It points directly to a pre-arranged plan of Lumumba to take complete control. Whatever the purpose of the plan, a main result of the upheaval it stimulated was that the United Nations ensured that all Belgian troops left the Congo despite the appalling atrocities, particularly with regard to white women, that had been committed during the mutiny. It also resulted in the flight of thousands of missionaries, technicians and key personnel from the Congo. Lumumba came to the United States on July 28th, and at a Press conference in the United Nations stated that a few European women had been 'disturbed in their honour'. Later, despite the fact that the American Ambassador to the Congo, Mr. C. Timberlake, verified that missionaries had been raped, Lumumba denied it. The Belgian White Paper submitted by Monsieur L. Merchiers, Minister of Justice of Belgium, listed undoubted atrocities, rapings, and thuggery of all kinds.

The seizure of Katanga by Tshombe during the Lumumba-Kasavubu feud would appear at this stage to be the only rational act of the whole nightmare. Seeing the rapid disintegration of the economy and realising the need for a firm hand, Tshombe declared the province of Katanga a separate and independent state with himself in supreme control. However, one of the surprising aspects of his quest for power was his unwillingness to talk to 'strong man Mobutu' when the latter seized the government.

The taking over of Katanga introduced a fresh element to the whole Congo episode. Tshombe, realising what was going on in Leopoldville and in other parts of the country due to the complete breakdown of the administration and the expulsion of the Belgians, decided to hold on not only to Belgian troops but also to Belgian technicians. There is no doubt that, unplanned though it was, the Belgians seized this last-minute opportunity as a means of salvaging some of their economic interests. At the same time it must in fairness be recognised that they made an honest effort to find a solution for the rapidly deteriorating Congolese situation. However, that too, so far as the military side was concerned, failed because the United Nations insisted on the withdrawal of the Belgian troops.

As soon as the situation became serious the Secretary-General of the United Nations sent out Dr. Ralph J. Bunche as his personal representative. Bunche was dictator without portfolio but his instructions were that his voice was only to be raised on extra-constitutional matters. Bunche remained in the Congo until September 1st, when he was replaced by Ambassador Rajeshwar Dayal. The whole activity of the United Nations in the Congo has been so lacking in precedent and the subject of so many complex problems that it is dealt with in a special chapter. The onus on the United Nations not to take any side in the internal conflict, coupled with the inability of the conflicting parties to solve their own problems, presents a general picture of impossible muddle.

As soon as the atrocities against the civilians had ceased, numbers of Belgian civilians started to drift back to the Congo. Many of these went at the personal invitation of Tshombe, Mobutu, and Kasavubu. As a result of this influx, Dayal, in his report to the United Nations dated November 2nd, declared : 'At the heart of the present confusion and disintegration in the Congo is the complete lack of progress in the way of political settlement, clearly a matter for the Congolese people themselves, which could provide a stable and recognised government and allow the assistance provided by the United Nations to be increasingly and more effectively applied.

'The various contenders for political power are still at a complete stalemate, and no effective, constitutional government exists to give direction to the solution of the nation's urgent problems.'

Having clearly stated that no central government existed Dayal, while recognising that a strong provincial government existed in Katanga, made a scathing attack on the Belgian Government because of the return of the Belgian personnel. Despite the fact that in his report to the United Nations he declared : 'The withdrawal of Belgian troops from Katanga, with the sole exception of technical personnel temporarily required at Kamina base, has been completed,' and also despite the knowledge that all Belgians in Katanga were there at the express invitation of the provincial government, nevertheless he reported that 'a gradual but purposeful return is being staged by Belgian nationals, which has assumed serious significance in view

of the key areas which they have penetrated in the public
life of the country, and the possible effect of their activities
on all aspects of the United Nations' responsibilities. All
too often these developments have coincided with anti-
United Nations policies or feelings at the various points of
impact. Belgian activities in recent weeks have increased
the intransigence of the United Nations command as well
as of the Katangese authorities, inhibited peaceful political
activity and therefore the possibility of an eventual return
to constitutional government and the re-establishment of
the unity and integrity of the country.'

Dag Hammarskjold supported the Dayal Report while
James J. Wadsworth, chief United States delegate, declared
that the Belgian Government was helping rather than
hindering the situation in the Congo. In the meantime,
Monsieur Pierre Wigny, Belgian Foreign Minister, launched
a scathing attack on the United Nations, declaring that its
functionaries did not exercise 'the rule of restrictions imposed on them by the protocol of public officials'. He again
confirmed that the Belgian officials in Katanga and in other
parts of the Congo were there by invitation and that the
United Nations had no mandate whatever which gave them
the right to expect that *all* technical aid to the ex-colony
should be channelled through them.

Following the Dayal Report, a Committee of Conciliation consisting of members of the Afro-Asian countries was
established to go to the Congo and endeavour to straighten
out by means of a round table conference the constitutional
scramble. Promptly President Kasavubu objected to this
procedure and came to New York to attend the United
Nations in person. His primary purpose in coming was to
clarify the situation with regard to the Congolese delegation
to the United Nations. After considerable discussion he and
those nominated by him were accepted as the official delegates. It was during this visit that fighting broke out in
Leopoldville because of the failure of the Ghanian

ambassador to the Congo to leave the country when requested by Mobutu. If anything, Ghana's interference
helped Kasavubu.

Although he and his delegates were found acceptable
to the United Nations, Kasavubu returned to the Congo on
November 24th without yet declaring that he found
the conciliation mission acceptable. At the very moment
when he was leaving New York, both United Nations and
Congolese troops were, as a result of the Congolese-Ghana
debacle, digging in in various parts of Leopoldville.

And so the situation remains unchanged. Four would-be
leaders—Kasavubu, Lumumba, Mobutu, and Tshombe—
hold the fate of the Congo in their hands. What happens
to the 14,000,000 Congolese people, judging from these
leaders' actions, seems of no importance. No progress of
any kind has been made constitutionally. Only one outstanding fact seems acceptable : At the time of writing these
words, there is no immediate prospect of a return to sanity,
or of the Congo setting up an effective government of its
own.

υ

Chapter Thirteen

THE UNITED NATIONS IN THE CONGO

ON July 13th, 1960 the Security Council of the United
Nations authorised the Secretary-General 'to take the
necessary steps, in consultation with the Government of
the Republic of the Congo, to provide the Government
with such military assistance as may be necessary until,
through the efforts of the Congolese Government with the
technical assistance of the United Nations, the national
security forces may be able, in the opinion of the Government, to meet fully their tasks'. This constitutes the mandate for the United Nations' activity in all its forms in the
Congo.

This is the first time in history that any international
organisation has had to face so difficult a task under almost
impossible circumstances. The United Nations in the Congo
is a neutral body; under no circumstances must it do anything that will interfere with the Congolese rival parties,
nor must it at any time favour any one of them. In his
first report to the United Nations, dated July 18th, 1960,
after his initial experience in the Congo, Hammarskjold
summed up his task as follows : 'Thus, the United Nations'
operation must be separate and distinct from activities by
any national authorities. Likewise, it follows from the rule
that the United Nations' units must not become parties in
internal conflicts, that they cannot be used to enforce any
specific political solution of pending problems or to influence the political balance decisive to such a solution.
Apart from the general reasons for this principle, there is
the specific one, that it is only on this basis that the United

97

Nations can expect to be able to draw on member countries for contributions in men and materials.'

Although the Secretary-General was daily made more aware of the complexity of the situation, it is obvious now that he did not immediately realise that it was to develop into one of the most crucial tests the United Nations has yet had to face.

Many of the leading personnel in the United Nations believe that, over the fifteen years of its existence, a powerful international 'mystique' has been developed, although nobody has yet given it any clear definition. There is little doubt that in Western Europe, and even behind the Iron Curtain, the strength and influence of this 'mystique' are important, but its application to an area of Africa like the Congo has shown that, in such a situation, its importance tends to be grossly overrated. What do the millions of Congolese know of this 'mystique'? What do they know of the United Nations? Frankly, they know nothing of the former and little of the latter. While quite a number of them may have heard of the United Nations, its function and purpose still mean very little to them. This fact, therefore, makes the United Nations' task particularly difficult, for although the United Nations is neither a government nor a controlling power of any kind, it has to operate behind the functional aura of both. It has an army which cannot fight unless to defend itself; it has diplomats who cannot act diplomatically in the traditional sense of the word, and it has advisors who can only advise within very narrow limits.

When Katanga seceded from the Congo Central Government, it became one of the more difficult tasks of the United Nations to ensure that the Belgians left their territory. The United Nations was in the Congo as the result of a specific request from the Congolese Central Government. Subsequently, the Congolese Central Government wished to supply various personnel to accompany United Nations' representatives visiting Katanga. This offer

had to be refused (see correspondence at Appendix III).
This was but one of the many situations which arose and
which turned the United Nations itself into a political
playground for the internal contestants as well as for those
external ones who also wished to influence the course of
events.

When the Congo crisis was brought initially before the
United Nations, Hammarskjold decided that Afro-Asian
representatives would best serve its interests in dealing with
the Congo situation. He therefore selected a group which
is for the most part African, but which has a strong Asian
content. However, since the African advisers come from
entirely different camps, the result has been to make the
Congo issue still more complicated by having their rival
African ideologies thrown into an already chaotic situation.

This divergence has brought to light a new and somewhat
serious development within the United Nations itself. It
must be realised—although many are reluctant to face this
fact—that many of the delegates from the new nations are
quite inexperienced, inadequately educated and, all too
often, possessed of only the most elementary knowledge of
world affairs. Yet these men are frequently the most vociferous when it comes to discussing policy. They make the
longest speeches and are responsible for the most emotional
and uncalled for outbursts.

Maturity in world affairs is something that takes time to
grow, so that there is ample excuse for the behaviour of
these delegates. On the other hand there is no point in
ignoring the fact that, although this inadequacy exists
and must be excused, it can and does have serious reper-
cussions in a situation like that existing in the Congo. In
his report to the United Nations on October 17th, Hammarskjold said : 'Much has been said in this debate regarding
the Congo, its problems and the United Nations' effort in
support of the independence, integrity, peace and progress
of the Congo. Much has been said which has been ill-
founded. Whether this has been the result of misinforma-

tion, of an emotional engagement or of tactical considerations but flimsily related to the interests of the Congo, I
leave to others to consider.' From this statement it would
seem the Secretary-General is fully aware of these short-
comings. To be aware of them is one thing; to find a way
whereby the United Nations can act without being unduly
influenced by them is another matter, and constitutes a
problem which that august body will have to face much
more seriously in the future.

The United Nations has been six months in the Congo.
It has something over 20,000 troops there and a number of
other personnel (see General Organisation of the United
Nations in the Congo at Appendix I). Politically, it has made
no progress whatever for the simple reason that it is not
by its mandate permitted to make, interfere in, or influence
any specific settlement. That must come from the Congolese
themselves and from them only. It has been helping
economically and endeavouring to assist certain industries
to carry on. Socially, it is endeavouring to find a sufficient
number of teachers and to establish an educational programme so that the Congo can, at least, begin laying the
foundation for the conduct of its own affairs in the future.
For this purpose it has recently circularised various governments in an effort to find 500 teachers and educational
advisers who are prepared to go to the Congo to work.

If the creation of a furore over its activities could be
considered the criterion of success, then the United Nations
has succeeded. If, on the other hand, it is the criterion of
failure, then the United Nations has failed in the Congo.
In the first place, practically all the political parties in the
Congo have in recent months demanded that the United
Nations leave the Republic, lock, stock and barrel. Even
Kasavubu, who has been duly appointed and recognised in
the United Nations itself as a delegate and the head of his
government, has severely criticised its activities, and up to
the end of November 1960 refused to allow a conciliatory
mission from it to go to the Congo. This seems all the more

ridiculous inasmuch as the United Nations is in the Congo and will obviously remain there until such time as there is a central government capable of carrying on the rule of law. Russia and her satellites have also demanded that it leave and have accused it of part of the Western powers and failing in its duties.

The real fact, of course, is that the Cold War has been brought to the Congo just as it was brought years ago to the conference rooms of the United Nations itself. Mr. Quaison-Sackey, Chief of the Ghana delegation to the United Nations, declared that the problem of the Cold War in the Congo is one of the four reasons why it is almost impossible for the United Nations to operate there. During the same debate, Mr. Brucan of the Rumanian delegation referring to a statement by the United States to the effect that it did not send military personnel and armaments to the Congo, said : 'This is indeed an unusual occasion for the United States to make much a statement in this Assembly. The reason is not a matter of principle but rather because the United States Government decided in this instance to depend entirely on the Secretary-General of the United Nations.'

Similar accusations have been levelled at the United Nations by practically every single nation behind the Iron Curtain. Denials have been made by all of those in the Western camp. This alone makes the United Nations' task doubly difficult, for three major deterrents to completely free United Nations' action in the Congo present themselves. First, there is the over-all problem of the internal political (and physically warring) combatants, each endeavouring to persuade the United Nations to espouse its own specific cause. Second, there is the external influence of a number of African powers each jockeying for a position of influence in the Congo of the future; third, there is the Congo as a political football in the Cold War with the United Nations' building as the playing field.

There is another, and even more important, aspect of

the United Nations' activity in the Congo. That is the financial cost of the whole business. The Congo at the present moment is virtually bankrupt and is therefore quite incapable of paying for itself. The United Nations expects to have to foot the bill, but, unfortunately, at the moment it has very little left in reserve with which to pay it. The Secretary-General, on October 24th, 1960, presented to the General Assembly supplementary estimates to cover this unexpected expense for the period between July to December 1960. The grand total comes to over $66,000,000. Even these estimates do not cover the cost of international financial aid to be provided for the purpose of restoring the economic life of the new Republic and carrying on its public services, including education, health and internal security.

To add to all the other difficulties in the Congo, the Russians so far have refused to make any further contribution on the grounds that the United Nations in the Congo is not fulfilling its true function and is merely a tool of the Western powers. Her satellites are adopting the same attitude. A number of the new nations, although more than vociferous, just cannot afford the kind of contribution that would normally be their share. It has therefore been suggested that the United States, already overburdened with financial aid, should contribute fifty per cent of the grand total, while Britain should pay much more than her fair share. The money will probably be forthcoming, but here again it will probably bring with it bitterness and a sense of righteous indignation and injustice.

In the meantime, if there is any hope for the Congo, the United Nations must carry on. It has made mistakes; it continues to make mistakes and will continue to make them. But the fact remains that if there is to be any salvation, it must come through the United Nations. Hammarskjold summed up the problem when speaking of the Congo on October 17th, 1960 : 'The end of all political effort must be the well-being of the individual in a life of safety and freedom. In the case of the Congo, as elsewhere, the means to this end are in the first place the independence, peace, integrity and prosperity of the country. In turn, this goal requires the maintenance and progress of economic life, the functioning of a good judiciary system, a soundly working administration, all under the responsibility of a government, stable, thanks to its firm roots in the free will of the people, expressed and developed in democratic forms. This is the perspective in which the effort of the United Nations must be seen. This perspective should determine our judgment and give us the sense of proportion necessary if we are to avoid substituting the means for the ends and the interests of the man or the group for those of the people.'

CHAPTER FOURTEEN

THE CONGO DISASTER AND AFRICA

DURING the second world war, Britain set up on the west coast of Africa an organisation called the West African Council. Its primary purpose was to co-ordinate the war effort of the British West African colonies. At that time, the Belgians in the Congo were in constant and close touch with the Council. The French in West Africa were in the Vichy camp until the Germans were driven out of North Africa; then they too joined the Allied cause.*

The Council remained in existence after the war, and had as its Director Sir Gerald Creasy, afterwards Governor of Gilbraltar. Its post-war purpose was to act as a liaison office between the West African territories and to help towards a solution of many of the health, education and other social problems common to them all. However, political events moved so quickly that it never really had an opportunity to fulfil its purpose, and by the time it was closed about five years ago it had become little more than a post office. Although the Council did not operate as was intended, it did achieve one important end. It demonstrated that the British Government was aware that the colonial powers faced common difficulties and that it ought to be possible to find common solutions. By the very nature of its work it was, during its post-war lifetime, in constant touch with the French and the Belgians, even

* The author was commanding the Fifth Battalion of the Nigeria Regiment which provided the guard of honour at the time, and was personally present when the first French delegation made a friendly visit to the Chief Commissioner in Kaduna (now the capital), Northern Nigeria.

though the latter ceased to be either very enthusiastic or
co-operative as soon as the war ended. The Council also
gave expression to a development that was steadily becoming more important, namely that, south of the Sahara,
Africa was ceasing to be a series of colonies each solely
concerned with its own particular problems. A common ideal
was gradually coming into existence amongst most of the
African peoples; it was the ideal of equality with the white
races. Prior to the recent catastrophe, the Belgians had
made every effort to isolate the Congo from this movement;
the Portugese still persist in attempts to do the same and
feel that they are succeeding. As for South Africa, the
nationalists have not succeeded in making the Bantus live
in an atmosphere free from politics, although they persist in
behaving as though they have.

As the ideal of racial equality took root and spread
through the African continent, it was nourished by the
achievements after liberation of the new African states, and
has now become a vital factor in African life. Problems,
hopes and ideals flowed together in common and, up to the
time of the Congo debacle, each successive development
went to the credit side of Africa's move to freedom.

What of the situation today? The Congo delivered a
worse blow to African pride than any African country or
individual has yet admitted. As far as the different colonial
policies are concerned it has pointed a clear distinction
between the successes and the failures, and has mitigated
very considerably the criticisms so often directed against
British colonialism. This does not mean that it has justified
colonialism. It has not; but it has clearly indicated the
minimum requirements for independence and even the most
biased of African leaders are fully aware of this lesson, even
if they refuse to acknowledge it openly.

Inasmuch as Ghana, on achieving independence, became
a political leading power south of the Sahara, it was
natural that the Congo disaster should have given Nkrumah
ideas about exercising and thus increasing his already high

prestige. His marriage to Guinea had proved a sad failure because of Touré's over-eagerness to flirt with the Communists. The Congo, however, gave him the opportunity to show that a group of south-of-the-Sahara African nations could deal with the Congo problems. It would not be unfair to Nkrumah to suggest that he had in mind the ideal leader of such a group—one Kwame Nkrumah. However, he overplayed his hand, and to such ill-effect that, during the Mobutu régime, the Ghana Embassy was closed and all its members asked to leave the country.

This action caused one of the major interim crises in the Congo for the Ghanian Ambassador, Mr. Nathaniel A. Welbeck, refused to go, declaring that Nkrumah had instructed him to remain. Ghana's attitude was that Mobutu had no authority to issue such a command. However, after considerable fighting between Congolese troops and United Nations forces who were guarding the Ghanian Embassy, Welbeck finally left. This incident showed that Ghana's interest in Congolese affairs was no mere passing phenomenon.

South Africa, which had passed through its first serious experience of racial rioting just prior to the Congo crisis, found in the latter an opposite (although by no means new) platform from which it could justify its policy of *apartheid*. The pathetic exhibition of so-called African leaders wallowing in their own inadequacy was just the kind of experience the Nationalist Government needed to justify its own near-slavery technique. What they failed to realise was their inability to prevent a similar tragedy in their own country when the South African natives seize the reins of power—as seize them they will.

There are two lessons to be learned from the Congo. The first is that, whether they are ready for it or not, the Africans must necessarily come to independence, and that, if they are unready, national disaster will inevitably follow. The second is that, in the light of modern events, there is only one way open to occupying powers in present colonial areas : to prepare their colonies for independence and to create as quickly as possible a healthy atmosphere of friendship and co-operation on which future economic, political and social relationships can be based. The Union of South Africa has accepted only the second half of the first lesson.

The position in Portugese Angola is even worse, for unless the Portugese have an immediate change of heart, it will soon find itself in just as sad a plight as the Congo. One could almost say 'worse', but it is difficult to visualise a situation worse than the Congolese chaos. There was a little secondary education in the Congo; there is practically none in the Portugese African territories. Catholicism in the Congo was powerful; in Angola and Mozambique it is *all*-powerful and has made no effort whatsoever to educate the Africans. The Portugese refuse to admit that they have colonies or that they are a colonial power. On the contrary, they say their overseas territories are merely an extension of Portugal itself, and that therefore they enjoy all that Portugese freedom entails. There is little room for such sophisms in the Africa of today.

Labour conditions in Angola are close to slavery. The country's economy is based on forced labour, and native delinquents who seek to avoid it, or who refuse to work, are flogged with the *palmatoria*. Basil Davidson describes this instrument in his book *The African Awakening* : 'It is a sort of mallet carved from one piece of hard wood, with a handle some ten or twelve inches long, the head being a disk some three inches across and an inch and a half thick. On each side of this disk five tapering holes were bored. These were in a pattern of the dots on the five of dice. The way this implement of torture was employed is this. The victim holds one hand out palm up. The operator brings the *palmatoria* with a sharp forceful blow on the outstretched palm. Under the force of the blow the flesh is sucked up into these tapering holes. The lessening diameter of the holes pinches the enclosed flesh and produces intense pain. The victim then presents the palm of the other hand

and the operator hits it. So the hands are struck alternately with a regular beat for the ordered number of blows.

The Rhodesias, and members of the future East African Federation proposed by Julius Nyerere, which would consist of Tanganyika, Kenya, Uganda, Zanzibar and Nyasaland, have all been watching the Congo attentively. Fortunately, both in East and Central Africa, where there is British influence, there are responsible leaders and little likelihood of a repetition of Congolese events. All the same, African leaders in these territories have made it quite clear that the failure of Belgian colonialism provides no sound reason for delaying their own movement towards independence. On the other hand, these same African leaders have been brought face to face with the consequences of irresponsibility, and it is to be hoped that, as Africans, they will be able to appreciate all that that entails.

The lessons of the Congo are not, however, confined to the Africans. The remaining colonial powers have much to learn, especially with regard to their traditional tardiness when action is urgent and imperative. Leading Africans have, for the most part, learned that successful independence is not simply a question of the withdrawal of the colonial power. The colonial powers must show that they too have learned their lessons. The pace of advancement in Kenya and Central Africa is still too slow and most people recognise it. These are only two of the areas where the situation calls for urgent measures.

Now that African nationalism is gathering force in its rush towards complete independence, the colonial powers must endeavour to keep up with it. One lesson from the Congo is that getting out is not an answer in itself; a second is that educative measures that will pave the way towards independence must be pressed forward without delay.

CHAPTER FIFTEEN

THE NEED FOR BENIGN AUTOCRACY

WHAT of the Congo's future? At this stage any answer to this question must obviously be speculative, all the more so because the unhappy country has now become the subject of international interest and intrigue. There are, however, certain predominating factors which, while they may be disregarded temporarily, must in the end contribute to the final settlement of the Congo Republic.

The United Nations must remain in the Congo a long time; years must elapse before the Congolese authorities, such as they are, can produce a sufficient number of qualified administrators to run their own land. The function of the United Nations up to the moment has been purely neutral, and events have shown that neutralism as a policy has none of the dynamism necessary to promote advancement. All energies have to be devoted to holding the ring against outside interference and avoiding identification with any of the internal contestants for power.

The primary cause of the tragedy which has brought the Congo to its present state of anarchy was the mutiny in the army. Since then, the army has disintegrated further and much of it is scattered through the bush. How, in a territory as vast as the Congo, can these men, who are trained to destroy not to build, be brought together or, at least, under control? Until that has been achieved they will prove a constant threat to any hope of peaceful development. Like the mercenaries of old, they will sell themselves to the highest bidder.

On the political side, and assuming that the threat from the army can be reduced, what of the future? One thing is almost certain : the reinstatement of Lumumba to any really influential position would be, for the Congo, disastrous. He has shown that he cannot be relied upon to carry out his promises, except possibly those he makes to the Russians. On the other hand, it would be foolish to disregard the fact that he still enjoys fairly considerable influence, especially with those who are associated with him in the National Congolese Movement.

Kasavubu has now been recognised as the Head of State, but it has still to be determined whether his control will emanate from the head of a central government or from the president of a federation. It is almost impossible, at this stage, to visualise any other form of constitution than a federal one. Tshombe of Katanga, businessman that he is, having had experience of what happens to the economy when rival leaders vie for power, is not likely willingly to return his province to the control of a central government. He could probably be prevailed upon to participate in a federal system. One cannot but sympathise with his point of view.

What of Mobutu? For a young and inexperienced man, he has displayed considerable tolerance, restraint and wisdom in coping with Leopoldville's immediate crises. He could have destroyed Lumumba; he deliberately spared him even though he was advised strongly to the contrary. Mobutu, considering the scarcity of potential leaders in the Congo, must have a part in its future.

What of the actual government? Too much is being and has been talked about democratic procedures in the Congo. The first thing to ensure is that the Congolese man-in-the-street or in-the-bush understands what democracy is all about. Until such time as he can be trained to understand this, he must, at the best, be subject to benign autocracy. Certain elements of democracy did exist in his tribal heritage. The Belgians were stupid and selfish enough to destroy that heritage and substituted for it their own particular form of paternalism. The latter, which really was a form of benign autocracy, must continue to be exercised but based on higher motives than those which inspired even the best Belgian régimes. This policy, when exercised for the right motives, can, however, easily be misinterpreted by those who have not an intimate knowledge of the African mind. It is impossible to destroy overnight African tradition and African heritage which have always demanded that the family, the village and the tribe be governed strongly. This is the only kind of rule that will command respect from the African people.

But who is to exercise it? Can the United Nations operate in this manner within the framework of its present mandate? The answer would appear to be 'no' and therefore, unless the General Assembly grants stronger powers and limited autocratic powers, there is little likelihood that a reasonable form of properly constituted government can be evolved from the appalling muddle of the present.

But even assuming that such additional power is granted to the United Nations administration, there are other vitally important considerations. One of the first is the time element. Years must elapse before an adequate number of Congolese are sufficiently well trained to accept administrative responsibility in their own country. Even then, when they do accept responsibility, a further period must elapse during which they must be helped over the mistakes of their own inexperience.

This raises the important question of future Belgo-Congolese relations. The economy of the Congo has been built on a foundation of Belgian capital, Belgian technical knowledge and Belgian personnel. Under the most ideal conditions, the introduction of other trained personnel from other countries would be less desirable, from a progressive point of view, than the retention of the Belgians. The latter understand the people, they understand the problems which are peculiar to the Congo, they understand the background to the progress already made, and—a small but possibly vital point—they speak the only European language the Congolese understand. If the Congo is to advance econom-

ically and speedily, something of the past, on which to build
for the future, must remain. The Congolese at the present
moment appear to be quite incapable of providing anything
which can be used as a firm foundation; so until such time
as they acquire the necessary skills, all aid must come from
outside and will have to be provided in arbitrary fashion.

Here again is the word 'arbitrary'. It will bear repetition
in this context, for even the best intentioned of anti-
colonialists and lovers of democracy cannot see the Congo's
future in any other terms. There is, however, one serious
danger. Can a pattern once established, in a place such as
the Congo, be changed for another when the time comes?
Here again, it is easy to pose the question, but, vital though
it is, no answer can be given.

A condition precedent is the reduction of international
intrigue to a minimum. And here a distinction must be
made between international intrigue and African intrigue
although they are both equally dangerous. The experience
of the last few months has shown that the African, on
attaining independence, is no different from his opposite
numbers in Europe. Nasser tried to grab Moslem leadership
in the African continent; Nkrumah is endeavouring to
extend his sphere of influence far beyond his own boundaries. There are leaders in Nigeria who have not yet shown
their hands simply because they have not had the time to
do so. One can only hope that they have learned from their
African colleagues the dangers of interference. Already one
of them is to head the conciliatory mission to the Congo—
that is if it ever goes there.

Out of all this one fact emerges : the solution to the
Congo's problems is not to be found amongst the traditional
patterns. There must be a new approach. In particular, it
must be realised that while the democracy of the West is
vital to the free world, some other system may prove to be
necessary, not only for the future of the Congo, but for the
future of the whole of Africa. If so, that system will have
to be accepted.

CONCLUSION

THE capture of Premier Lumumba in Port Franqui on 2 December, 1960 provoked a new crisis in the Congo and, instead of lessening the ex-Premier's status, confirmed him in the key rôle in the Congo's political turmoil.

The situation, since the completion of this book, has worsened in every respect. New names have been added to the list of those who are struggling for power. The United Nations, in its efforts to maintain neutrality and at the same time to keep the peace, has found that its position tends to become more and more untenable. Ghana, although threatening to withdraw its troops, has still maintained its intense interest and is still endeavouring to project itself as a leader in the field of African and international affairs. In Stanleyville, capital of Oriental Province, Prague-trained Antoine Gizenga, former vice-premier under Mr. Lumumba, has proclaimed Oriental Province a separate régime and is reputed to have a force of 7,000 armed men at his disposal. In Katanga, Lumumba forces have penetrated into the northern area and have been warring with President Tshombe. Lumumba forces have also taken control of Bakavu and most of the Province. These are the more important clashes, but they do indicate both the temper of the would-be leaders and a deteriorating situation which shows little hope of settlement.

All these events have been secondary to the arrest of Lumumba which has heightened the possibility of civil war. Since the early disintegration of authority tribal quarrels have been increasing daily with devastating effects both to the economic and sociological status of the country.

To add to all this, in January of 1961 the Soviet Union has endeavoured again to complicate the situation by bringing before the Security Council a charge that the Belgians, who are administering Ruanda Urundi, are using the trust territory as a springboard for aggressive operations against the Congo. The Soviet demanded that Ruanda Urundi be granted immediate independence.

In the Security Council the Russians referred to the presence of Mobutu's Congolese troops at the airport at Usumbura. Mr. Walter Loridan of Belgium replied as follows : 'As already reported in documents before the Council, the Belgian Government had not been informed in advance of the arrival of the Congolese contingent at the Usumbura airport at Ruanda Urundi. Faced with this *fait accompli*, the Belgian authorities had had no choice but to escort the Congolese contingent to the border, and that was what had been done. Any other action would have had much more serious consequences.' He also added that 'there were no Congolese soldiers in Ruanda Urundi, that any future unauthorised landing would be opposed, and that the Belgian Government had no intention of granting any such authorisation'.

The Soviet accusation failed to impress the Security Council, but of course the Russians intend to reopen the matter when the General Assembly meets on March 7. The fact that Mobutu troops were in Ruanda-Urundi (and there seems to be considerable haziness about the reason for their being there) is a decisive pointer to the chaotic state of the Congo and the irrational military antics of the leaders.

On 25 January, 1961, Kasavubu proposes to hold a round-table conference of Congolese political leaders. The belief that Lumumba may be released in order to attend this has many supporters and the January visit of Hammarskjold to the Congo was no doubt connected with this fact. One factor of some significance is the suggestion that, as Hammarskjold went to the Congo immediately following his meeting with President Kennedy (then President-Elect), the latter had advocated the release of Lumumba in the hope that his presence at such a conference would bring about some workable arrangement for peace and unity. By the time this book is in print, the answer to this speculation will be known.

While the Congolese leaders are struggling for personal power and prestige, starvation is rampant in the Congo. Thousands of people have died of hunger, and altogether the outlook for the coming year is quite terrifying. By the end of 1960 the United Nations had sent nearly 10,000,000 pounds of food, milk, and medical supplies to meet emergency needs, particularly those of refugees in tribal warfare areas, and to provide milk for a hundred thousand school children. Fourteen countries came to the aid of the famine-stricken people, but if complete disaster from famine is to be avoided this aid must be increased considerably; at the time of writing, official reports say that 200 people are dying daily from starvation. The United Nations has arranged to fly shipments of seed corn as well as actual foods to the stricken areas, while President Eisenhower is reported to be setting aside $5,000,000 for special aid.

Events occur speedily in the Congo. To date there have been few that give cause for encouragement. By the time this book is published perhaps there will be some light on the Congo's dark horizon and this bewildered and lost African child will have some hope of security and unity for the future.

APPENDIX I

GENERAL ORGANISATION

United Nations Headquarters (UNHQ) and
The United Nations in the Congo (ONUC)

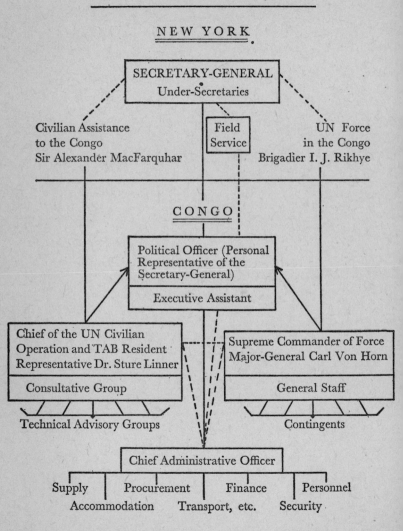

NEW YORK

SECRETARY-GENERAL
Under-Secretaries

Civilian Assistance
to the Congo
Sir Alexander MacFarquhar

Field
Service

UN Force
in the Congo
Brigadier I. J. Rikhye

CONGO

Political Officer (Personal
Representative of the
Secretary-General)

Executive Assistant

Chief of the UN Civilian
Operation and TAB Resident
Representative Dr. Sture Linner

Consultative Group

Technical Advisory Groups

Supreme Commander of Force
Major-General Carl Von Horn

General Staff

Contingents

Chief Administrative Officer

Supply   Procurement   Finance   Personnel

Accommodation   Transport, etc.   Security

CIVILIAN OPERATIONS

Chief of the UN Civilian Operation and TAB Resident
Representative

Deputy

Chief Assistant

	Consultative Group
1. Agriculture	6. Health
2. Communications	7. Instruction (national security forces)
3. Education	8. Labour market
4. Finance	9. Magistrature
5. Foreign trade	10. Natural resources and industry
	11. Public administration

Technical Advisory Groups

Agriculture	*Communications*	*Education*	*Finance*	*Foreign trade*	*Health*
Consultant	Consultant	Consultant	Consultant	Consultant	Consultant
Assistant	Assistant	—	Assistant	Assistant	Assistant
—	—	Technical	—	—	—
Technical	Technical	Experts	Technical	Technical	Technical
Experts	Experts		Experts	Experts	Experts

Instruction	*Labour market*	*Magistrature*	*Natural resources and industry*	*Public administration*
Consultant	Consultant	Consultant	Consultant	Consultant
—	Assistant	Assistant	Assistant	—
Technical	—	—	—	Technical
Experts	Technical	Technical	Technical	Experts
	Experts	Experts	Experts	

APPENDIX II

The following chronological background notes indicate some of the problems in the Congo. For the most part they have become more acute during recent months.

30 June 1960   A message from Secretary-General Dag Hammarskjold congratulating the Republic of the Congo on its attainment of independence on 30 June 1960.

1 July 1960   A cable from the Prime Minister of the Republic of the Congo, Patrice Lumumba, to the Secretary General requested admission to membership in the United Nations.

5 July 1960   A letter to the Secretary-General, expressing the Belgian Government's support for the admission of the Republic of the Congo to United Nations membership.

7 July 1960   The Security Council at its 872nd meeting adopted a resolution recommending to the General Assembly the Republic of the Congo's admission to membership in the United Nations.

12 July 1960   The Secretary-General met, at his request, with the heads of nine African delegations (Ethiopia, Ghana, Guinea, Liberia, Libya, Morocco, Sudan, Tunisia, United Arab Republic) to brief them on needs for United Nations assistance likely to arise in the Republic of the Congo.

12 July 1960   A cable from the President (Joseph Kasa-

buvu) and the Prime Minister (Patrice Lumumba) of
the Republic of the Congo to the Secretary-General
requested 'urgent dispatch' of United Nations military
assistance.

It said that the dispatch of metropolitan Belgian
troops to the Congo was in violation of the treaty of
friendship between Belgium and the Congo; that 'the
unsolicited Belgian action' was 'an act of aggression';
and that the essential purpose of the military aid
requested from the United Nations is 'to protect the
national territory of the Congo against the present
external aggression which is a threat to international
peace'.

13 July 1960 Addressing the Security Council at a night
meeting, the Secretary-General asked the Council to
act 'with utmost speed' on the request for military aid
from the Republic of the Congo. The only 'sound and
lasting solution' of the country's problem, he said, lay
in the government's own 'regular instruments', including its security administration, and technical assistance
was being planned, as requested.

15 July 1960 First troops of the United Nations' force,
from Ghana and Tunisia, arrived in the Congo.

19 July 1960 A meeting held in the Congo between Dr.
Ralph J. Bunche, the Belgian Ambassador, the Belgian
Army Chief of Staff and the Commanding General of
Belgian Forces.

19 July 1960 A U.S.S.R. letter, circulated as a Security
Council document, called for the immediate withdrawal of United States Army communications personnel reported by a news agency to be in the Congo.

20 July 1960 Representatives of the Republic of the
Congo arrived for meetings of the Security Council.

20 July 1960 Addressing the Security Council at a night
meeting the Secretary-General commented that 'the
United Nations has embarked on its biggest single

effort under United Nations colours, organised and
directed by the United Nations itself'.

23 July 1960 The Secretary-General announced that he
had received direct word from Dr. Ralph J. Bunche
that the evacuation of Belgian troops from Leopoldville had been fully completed at 6 p.m. on 23 July, in
full conformity with the agreement on this subject.

24 July 1960 Premier Patrice Lumumba of the Republic
of the Congo arrived at the United Nations.

26 July 1960 A communique was issued stating that on
24, 25 and 26 July, the Secretary-General and Premier
Lumumba held three meetings. Mr. Lumumba was
accompanied by Joseph Kasongo, President of the
Chamber of Representatives; Joseph Okito, Vice-Presi-
dent of the Senate; Thomas Kanza, Minister Delegate
at the United Nations; Andre Mandi, Secretary of
State in the Ministry of Foreign Affairs; and Bernard
Salumu, Private Secretary to the Prime Minister.

The communique stated that the Prime Minister
informed the Secretary-General of 'the wish of
the Congolese Government and Parliament, expressed
in decisions of these organs, that the Belgian
troops withdraw immediately from the whole of the
territory of the Republic'. He 'stressed with insistence
that the re-establishment of peace in the Congo was
conditioned on the immediate departure of Belgian
troops'.

20 August 1960 Lumumba condemned the 'personal
activity of the Secretary-General of the United
Nations'; demanded the 'immediate withdrawal of the
white troops which have provoked the latest incidents
and whose intentions towards the Republic are
obviously hostile'.

21 August 1960 In a letter to the Secretary-General Vasily
V. Kuznetsov, First Deputy Minister for Foreign
Affairs of the U.S.S.R., enclosed a statement by his

government on the situation in the Republic of the
Congo.

The statement pointed out that 'compelled to withdraw from a number of areas in the country, the
Belgian troops are being massed in Katanga', and that
'contrary to the assurances of the Secretary-General . . .
a detachment of soldiers from Canada—Belgium's
NATO ally—landed in Leopoldville a few days ago,
arousing the fully justified indignation of the Congolese people and giving rise to a further aggravation of
tension in the country'.

21 August 1960 Speaking to the Council, the Secretary-
General noted that the actions and attitudes of the
United Nations, and of himself in particular, had come
under 'severe criticism' from the Prime Minister of the
Congo, and that this criticism had been followed by a
series of actions against officials in the service of the
United Nations which 'gave an impression of deep
distrust and hostility fomented for political ends' and
'were of a nature to call for a formal and serious
protest'.

23 August 1960 The United Nations agreed to place
$5,000,000 at the disposal of the Republic of the
Congo to assist it in meeting its most immediate needs
for the import of merchandise. The counterpart in
Congolese francs will be used to meet current budget-
ary expenditures such as salaries of officials and relief
allocations.

29 August 1960 Dr. Bunche categorically denied allegations that Belgians had worn United Nations uniforms.
Regarding the problem of misuse of United Nations
armbands, he said that identity cards had been issued,
as in other missions, to be used in conjunction with
United Nations armbands.

1 September 1960 Dr. Bunche reported, 'We have the
Belgian troops out of the country . . .'

1 September 1960 In summing up his experiences in the

Congo, Dr. Bunche expressed belief that 'there has
never been in the history of international organisation
the spirit of co-operation amongst all the organisations
—the United Nations, the specialised agencies and
indeed private institutions as well—that has been
evidenced out there in these last two months', and
never before had there been 'so generous a response on
the part of the nations of the world, large and small',
to an appeal for aid.

5 September 1960   In a radio broadcast from Leopoldville,
President Joseph Kasavubu deposed Premier Lumumba, replacing him with Joseph Ileo, President of
the Congo Senate. President Kasavubu said Premier
Lumumba 'had plunged the nation into fratricidal
warfare'. Premier Lumumba broadcast an appeal to
the Congo army to stand by him against President
Kasavubu and U.N., and indicated that he was re-
moving President Kasavubu from his office as Chief of
State.

7 September 1960   The Chamber of Deputies voted 60–19
to 'invalidate' both the dismissal of Premier Lumumba
by President Kasavubu and the subsequent dismissal
of the President by the Premier.

At a news conference, President Eisenhower took 'a
very serious view' of the actions of the Soviet Union
in unilaterally aiding the Congo Government. He said
the main responsibility in the Congo was given to the
U.N. 'as the only organisation able to act without
adding to the risks of spreading conflict'.

8 September 1960   The Congo Senate voted 41 to 2, with
6 abstaining and 29 absent, against President Kasavubu's dismissal of Premier Lumumba.

10 September 1960   President Kasavubu informed the
Secretary-General of the composition of the new
Government at Leopoldville; 'The only lawful and
legal government is that consisting of Mr. Ileo, Prime
Minister'. He asked that the U.N. should not deal with

Lumumba, and requested that it should continue assistance and guard airports. He promised the U.N. full and complete co-operation.

Premier Lumumba wrote to the Secretary-General saying that the 'statement just made by the Secretary-General of the United Nations to the Security Council, that Mr. Kasavubu had the right to dismiss the Government only confirms' U.N. interference. He accused the Secretary-General of running counter to sovereign decisions taken by the Congolese Parliament.

13 September 1690 Colonel Mobutu announced that the Army would take over the reins of government until 1 January, 1961. He said : 'This is not a *coup d'état*'. In taking over, Colonel Mobutu said that Soviet, Czechoslovak and 'other Socialist' embassies and their technicians would have to leave.

18 September 1960 The U.S.S.R. recalled the Soviet Embassy staff, but declared that the U.S.S.R. would retain friendly relations with the Congo despite the withdrawal 'temporarily' of the diplomatic mission. It said that the lawful government (Lumumba Government) had been removed and a 'puppet régime obedient to foreigners' installed. The Ambassador of Czechoslovakia left also.

20 September 1960 A fifteen-member 'College of High Commissioners' was installed by Colonel Mobutu to act as a caretaker government; it was composed of students and young university graduates. Colonel Mobutu instructed the group to take over the administration from President Kasavubu. He declared that no other body was entitled to carry out government functions.

28 October 1960 Eight nations sponsor a Resolution before the General Assembly of the U.N. to seat representatives of Premier Lumumba and to reconvene Parliament. (They were Ceylon, Ghana, Guinea,

India, Indonesia, Mali, Morocco, and United Arab Republic.)

10 November 1960 A Resolution of the General Assembly was passed saying :

'The Credentials Committee recommends that the General Assembly accept the credentials of the representatives of the Republic of the Congo issued by the Head of State (Kasavubu) and communicated by him to the President of the General Assembly in a letter dated November 8, 1960.'

15 November 1960 President Kasavubu in New York, notified the Secretary-General that he did not accept the proposal to dispatch to the Congo a Conciliation Commission. He proposed a 'Summit' meeting on the Congo of 25 independent African States.

16 November 1960 Colonel Mobutu's army arrested Lovelace Mensah, member of the Ghana Embassy in Leopoldville, accusing him of seeking to provide help for Premier Lumumba.

18 November 1960 Colonel Mobutu's régime announced that the Congo had severed diplomatic relations with Ghana, accusing Ghana of meddling in Congo affairs.

19 November 1960 Ghanaian diplomat, Nathaniel A. Welbeck, ordered to leave the Congo within 48 hours. Ghana Embassy guarded by U.N. Force.

21 November 1960 In Leopoldville, Congolese Army units clashed with U.N. Tunisian troops guarding the Ghana Embassy. Several were killed and many wounded when Colonel Mobutu's army moved to expel forcibly diplomat Nathaniel A. Welbeck, previously ordered out of Congo. President Kasavubu, in New York, sent regrets to the President of Tunisia and an explanation to the Secretary-General.

The Secretary-General warned the General Assembly that U.N. finances were at a critical point. He said that the U.N. must withdraw Congo forces unless 'not less than $20 million' was raised by the end of 1960.

He estimated Congo costs for 1960 at $66,625,000. By the end of 1961 costs would be $150 million to $200 million.

22 November 1960   The Ghanaian Government acceded to Colonel Mobutu's demand that Nathaniel A. Welbeck should leave the Congo. Fighting between U.N. troops and Colonel Mobutu's soldiers subsided on his departure.

1 December 1960   President Kasavubu broke off relations with the United Arab Republic and asked the Ambassador to leave Leopoldville. In a letter to President Gamal Abdul Nasser, he declared that United Arab Republic Representatives 'have been sustaining rebel elements and hatching plots'.

2 December 1960   Colonel Mobutu announced that gendarmes under his command had arrested Premier Lumumba in Port Franqui.

APPENDIX III

The surfeit of correspondence which has resulted from the Congo crisis has made it impossible to present anything suggestive of a condensed but comprehensive résumé. The following excerpts are intended to highlight some of the more interesting but acute difficulties of the whole situation.

I

Letter dated 15 August 1960 from the Secretary-General of the United Nations addressed to Mr. Patrice Lumumba, Prime Minister of the Republic of the Congo.

Leopoldville

Sir,

I have received your letter of today's date. In it I find allegations against the Secretary-General as well as objections to the Secretary-General's interpretation of the resolutions with the implementation of which he has been entrusted. In your letter you also submit certain requests which appear to derive from a position contrary to my interpretation of the resolutions.

There is no reason for me to enter into a discussion here either of those unfounded and unjustified allegations or of the interpretation of the Security Council's resolutions. As the letter is an official communication I shall have it circulated today as a Security Council document. Should the Security Council consider it necessary to take a stand with

regard to the action which I have taken or to my interpretation of its decisions, I am prepared to submit my
comments in person at a Council meeting. I hope that if
such a meeting is convened you too will see fit to present
your case to the Council in person. As far as the actions
requested by you are concerned, I shall naturally follow
the instructions which the Council may find it necessary or
useful to give me.

I note that you do not mention my letter of yesterday
evening to the Minister of Foreign Affairs requesting an
opportunity to report to the Government of the Republic
of the Congo on the implementation of the Security
Council's resolutions. I am still awaiting a reply to this
proposal. My letter of yesterday to the Minister of Foreign
Affairs and this reply will be included among the documents circulated to the Security Council.

I have the honour to be, etc.

(*Signed*) DAG HAMMARSKJOLD

*Letter dated 15 August 1960 from Mr. Lumumba, Prime
Minister of the Republic of the Congo, addressed to the
Secretary-General of the United Nations.*

Leopoldville

Sir,

I have the honour to acknowledge receipt of your letter
of today's date. The letter I addressed to you on 14 August
1960 on behalf of the Government of the Republic of the
Congo contains no allegations against the Secretary-General
of the United Nations but rather reveals facts which should
be made known to the Security Council and to the world
at large. The Government of the Republic is perfectly well
aware that the positions you have adopted are in no sense
those of the Security Council, in which it continues to have
confidence. It is paradoxical to note that it was only after
making arrangements with Mr. Tshombe and the Belgians
surrounding him that you decided to inform the Govern-

ment of the Republic. Furthermore, you at no time considered it advisable to consult the Government of the Republic as the resolution of the Security Council recommended you to do. The Government considers that you refused to give it the military assistance it needs and for which it approached the United Nations. I should be grateful if you would inform me in clear terms whether you reject the specific proposals contained in my letter of 14 August 1960.

In expectation of an immediate reply, I have the honour to be, etc.

(*Signed*) P. LUMUMBA
Prime Minister

Letter dated 15 August 1960 from the Secretary-General of the United Nations addressed to Mr. Lumumba, Prime Minister of the Republic of the Congo.

Leopoldville

Sir,

I received your letter of 15 August in reply to my letter of the same date. I presume that your letters have been approved by the Council of Ministers and that you will inform the Council of Ministers of my replies. I have nothing to add to my reply to your first communication dated 14 August and received today at noon. Your letter will be circulated to the Security Council immediately at my request. If the Council of Ministers takes no initiative which compels me to change my plans or has no other specific proposal to make, I shall go to New York this evening in order to seek clarification of the attitude of the Security Council.

You must have observed that the information on the deployment of the United Nations Force in Katanga shows that what you have said on this subject is erroneous. You must also have observed that the memorandum on the interpretation of paragraph 4 of the resolution of 9 August has been submitted to the Security Council and that no

member of the Council has taken the initiative of question-
ing its validity.

I have the honour to be, etc.

(*Signed*) DAG HAMMARSKJOLD

*Letter dated 15 August 1960 from Mr. Lumumba, Prime
Minister of the Republic of the Congo, addressed to the
Secretary-General of the United Nations.*

Leopoldville

Sir,

I have just this moment received your letter of today's
date in reply to the one I sent you an hour ago. Your letter
does not reply at all to the specific questions or concrete
proposals contained in my letters of 14 and 15 August.
There is nothing erroneous in my statements, as you maintain. It was because I publicly denounced, at a recent press
conference, your manœuvres in sending to Katanga only
troops from Sweden—a country which is known by public
opinion to have special affinities with the Belgian Royal
family—that you have suddenly decided to send African
troops into that province.

If no member of the Security Council has taken the
initiative to question the validity of your Memorandum and
your plans of action it is because the members of the
Council do not know exactly what is going on behind the
scenes. Public opinion knows—and the members of the
Security Council also know—that after the adoption of the
last resolution you delayed your journey to the Congo for
twenty-four hours solely in order to engage in talks with
Mr. Pierre Wigny, Belgian Minister of Foreign Affairs,
administrator of mining companies in the Congo and one
of those who plotted the secession of Katanga.

Before leaving New York for the Congo, the Congolese
delegation, led by Mr. Antoine Gizenga, Vice President of
the Council, urgently requested you to contact my Government immediately upon your arrival in Leopoldville and
before going to Katanga—this, in conformity with the

5—TC

Security Council's resolution of 14 July 1960. I personally laid particular stress on this point in the letter I sent to you on 12 August through the intermediary of your Special Representative, Mr. Ralph Bunche. Completely ignoring the legal Government of the Republic, you sent a telegram from New York to Mr. Tshombe, leader of the Katanga rebellion and emissary of the Belgian Government. Mr. Tshombe, again at the instigation of the Belgians placed at his side, replied to this telegram stipulating two conditions for the entry of United Nations troops into Katanga. According to the revelations just made by Mr. Tshombe at his press conference, you entirely acquiesced in the demands formulated by the Belgians speaking through Mr. Tshombe.

In view of all the foregoing, the Government and people of the Congo have lost their confidence in the Secretary-General of the United Nations. Accordingly we request the Security Council today to send immediately to the Congo a group of observers representing the following countries : Morocco, Tunisia, Ethiopia, Ghana, Guinea, the United Arab Republic, Sudan, Ceylon, Liberia, Mali, Burma, India, Afghanistan and Lebanon. The task of these observers will be to ensure the immediate and entire application of the Security Council resolutions of 14 and 22 July and 9 August 1960.

I earnestly hope that the Security Council, in which we place our full confidence, will grant our legitimate request. A delegation of the Government will accompany you, in order to express its views to the Security Council. I would therefore ask you kindly to delay your departure by twenty-four hours in order to permit our delegation to travel on the same aircraft.

I have the honour to be, etc.

(*Signed*) P. LUMUMBA
Prime Minister

II

Letter dated 18 August 1960 from Mr. Bunche addressed to the Prime Minister of the Republic of the Congo, Mr. Lumumba.

Sir,

I have the honour to draw your attention to an extremely serious incident which occurred in the grounds of your residence late at night on 17 August.

At about 11.30 p.m. last night I sent two United Nations security officers to your residence to deliver my reply to your letter to me of 17 August regarding the members of the National Assembly who wish to return to Katanga for their vacation. These two officers, one of whom wore United Nations uniform and the other civilian dress, drove to your residence in a white United Nations jeep. Both are United Nations officials of long standing. On arrival at the door of your residence, they explained to the Congolese gendarmes on guard that they wished to deliver a letter from me. They were asked to show their identity cards, which they did. In spite of that, the gendarmes arrested them and led them behind the residence where they took their weapons, wallets, watches and rings. They even threatened to shoot them and would have done so had it not been for the intervention of the Ghanaian guards. To secure their release I had to send General Rikhye to your residence and from there to the offices of the Second Company of Military Police at Camp Leopold. Our two officers were released, but a watch and a wallet containing 9,000 Congolese francs belonging to one of them were not returned and about 6,000 francs had been removed from the wallet of the other.

After General Rikhye had returned with the two officers I asked my deputy, Mr. Liu, to telephone General Lundula who had given us a garbled account of the incident a little earlier, to inform him of the details of this deplorable occurrence and to express our indignation.

We as members of the United Nations came to your country, Mr. Prime Minister, in response to your urgent appeal. We came as friends. We are your guests. We are therefore entitled to expect that your Government will protect us, while we are negotiating with it, from outrages such as those committed last night in the very grounds of your residence. As the senior United Nations official here, I am responsible for protecting from any form of abuse the very large number of people who from the remotest parts of the world responded to the appeals addressed to them by the United Nations in your interest. I trust, and I should appreciate your confirmation of this point, that those responsible for the outrages committed in the grounds of your residence will be severely punished and that a serious attempt will be made to recover and return to their rightful owners the watch and money which were lost. What is still more important, however, is of course an assurance that your Government will take effective action to prevent a recurrence of such incidents in the future.

I transmit to you herewith the letter which our two officers were unable to deliver to you and which was also taken from them by the Congolese guards at the door of your residence.

I have the honour to be, etc.

(*Signed*) RALPH J. BUNCHE

III

Letter dated 24 August 1960 from the Permanent Representative of Belgium addressed to the Secretary-General.

I have the honour to refer to my letter of 20 August in which I informed you that the withdrawal of Belgian troops from the Congo would be effected within a maximum period of eight days.

Acting upon the request made to me yesterday by your aide Mr. Wieschhoff, I am in a position to confirm to you, on behalf of my Government, that the Belgian troops will in fact have withdrawn from the Congo before 2400 hours, 29 August.

I wish to add that the small contingent of Belgian troops still at Albertville (Katanga) will be evacuated before today is over. The help of the United States' aircraft offered Belgium through your intermediary will be required to effect the total withdrawal of the troops.

The Belgian Government requests your support in enabling the Sabena aircraft which are in the Congo to be used for transportation into the interior of the Congo.

I have the honour to be, etc.

(*Signed*) WALTER LORIDAN
Permanent Representative of Belgium

P.S. As I signed this letter I learned that the Belgian troops have left Albertville.

Note Verbale *of 29 August 1960 from the Secretary-General addressed to the Permanent Representative of Belgium.*

The Secretary-General presents his compliments to the Permanent Representative of the Belgian Government to the United Nations and wishes to draw his attention to the following facts :

In a letter dated 20 August the Representative gave the Secretary-General the assurance that the withdrawal of the Belgian troops would be effected within a maximum period of eight days. Subsequently, in a letter dated 24 August, the Representative confirmed, on behalf of his Government, that the Belgian troops would in fact have left the Congo before 2400 hours on 29 August.

In reply to a request addressed to the Secretary-General's Representative at Elisabethville for precise information concerning the situation prevailing in Katanga at 2400 hours on 29 August the Secretary-General has just been informed as follows :

Because of communications difficulties, details concerning

the situation at Albertville and Kamina have not been received. It appears, however, that one company and troops of the Headquarters Staff are still at Elisabethville and that a like number of troops are at Kamina, awaiting their departure. Also, the rear-guard of a paratroop battalion at Albertville expects to embark tomorrow morning.

The Secretary-General wishes to draw the Government's attention to this information, which he hopes is unfounded. He would be grateful if the Government would give him precise information concerning the situation prevailing at the expiry of the term indicated by the Representative for the evacuation of the troops.

Letter dated 30 August 1960 from the Permanent Representative of Belgium addressed to the Secretary-General.

I have the honour to inform you that the withdrawal of Belgian troops in the Congo has been completed with the sole exception of some members of the First Paratroop Battalion who are in transit at Albertville, awaiting a vessel which should arrive momentarily to transport them to Usumbura. Instructions have been issued to the effect that, should it be necessary and in order to avoid any delay, they should be evacuated by air. Thus the withdrawal of Belgian troops from the Congo has in effect been completed.

I shall not fail to inform you as soon as I have been advised of the departure of the last troops.

I have the honour to be, etc.

(*Signed*) WALTER LORIDAN
Permanent Representative of Belgium

Note verbale dated 30 August 1960 from the Secretary-General addressed to the Permanent Representative of Belgium.

The Secretary-General of the United Nations presents his compliments to the Permanent Representative of Belgium and wishes to inform him as follows :

In a *note verbale* dated 29 August 1960 the Secretary-

General expressed the desire to receive from the Belgian Government precise information concerning the situation with regard to the evacuation of Belgian troops at the expiry of the term indicated in its letters of 20 and 24 August for their evacuation.

In reply to that note the Secretary-General has today received a letter informing him that the withdrawal of Belgian troops from the Congo has been completed with the sole exception of some members of the First Paratroop Battalion who are in transit at Albertville awaiting a vessel which should arrive momentarily to transport them to Usumbura. The withdrawal of Belgian troops from the Congo, the Representative states, has thus in effect been completed.

The Secretary-General has, however, just received a report from his representatives who arrived at Kamina today, 30 August, at 1430 hours local time. At that time Belgian combat troops consisting of one 400-man battalion of paratroopers, one 120-man company of airfield guards and one school of aviation comprising fifty instructors and students had not yet been evacuated. The Secretary-General's representatives have been informed that it is proposed to evacuate seventy men on the evening of 30 August and thirty-nine men on 31 August by air and that the rest are to be evacuated by rail on 1 and 2 September and subsequently by ship from Albertville on 3 and 4 September.

The Secretary-General expresses his surprise at finding that there is a marked difference between the information received from Brussels and the facts observed on the scene. He finds it necessary to stress that the presence of large Belgian military units, contrary to the assurances given by the Belgian Government, is certain to arouse sharp criticism. The United Nations based itself on the assurances received and did everything to facilitate the evacuation. As the evacuation has, nevertheless, not yet been completed the Secretary-General deems it necessary to submit a formal protest to the Belgian Government requesting that the evacuation of Belgian troops which are still in the Congo should be effected immediately.

The Secretary-General considers it necessary to submit a report to the Security Council concerning the situation.

IV

Letter dated 3 August 1960 from the Secretary-General addressed to the Deputy Prime Minister of the Republic of the Congo.

I have received your letter of 3 August 1960 in which you inform me that 'the *Conseil du Cabinet du Vice-Premier Ministre* has decided to attach to Dr. Bunche, for his journey to Katanga, three members of the Government . . . escorted by twenty Ghanaian soldiers'.

May I point out to you that a proposal to the effect that representatives of the Government should accompany Dr. Bunche was made by you the day before yesterday, when I met the small Committee. You will remember that I then explained that I could not accept such a proposal; and I must maintain that position. Your proposal was not re-peated yesterday when I announced to you Dr. Bunche's departure. In this respect I have to tell you again that the mission of Dr. Bunche is purely a United Nations mission, the character of which should not be compromised by the arrangements made.

With regard to the Ghanaian military escort, the princi-ples established by the Security Council resolution reserve for decision by the Secretary-General and, under him, of the Commander, any military dispositions regarding the Force. The dispatch of the Ghanaian group would not be in line with the plans made and announced.

I have the honour to be, etc.

(*Signed*) DAG HAMMARSKJOLD
Secretary-General

Letter dated 3 August 1960 from the Deputy Prime Minister of the Republic of the Congo addressed to the Secretary-General.

Further to the letter which I have addressed to you today, I have the honour to confirm that Mr. Bunche will have to be accompanied on his journey to Katanga by three members of the Government of the Republic of the Congo.

I have also deemed it necessary to attach a Government journalist to them.

I should be grateful if you would meet me at my office on the morning of Thursday, 4 August 1960, before the first United Nations mission led by Mr. Bunche leaves for Katanga, so that we can arrange the details of the journey.

I have the honour to be, etc.

(*Signed*) A. GIZENGA
Deputy Prime Minister

Letter dated 3 August 1960 from the Secretary-General addressed to the Deputy Prime Minister of the Republic of the Congo.

I have duly received the letter which you sent me on the evening of 3 August.

As you doubtless already know from my letter which was sent to you somewhat earlier this evening, the arrangements for Dr. Bunche's journey have already been made and I shall not alter them. You will certainly appreciate that the composition of a United Nations mission is determined by the Secretary-General alone.

Should you wish to have an exchange of views on the arrangements made, I shall be at your disposal at the Royal Palace tomorrow morning, at any time that will suit you. But I must warn you that that must not and cannot delay the arrangements for the journey.

In view of the possibility that my letter in reply to your first communication on this subject, which I sent by special messenger to your home, may not have reached you, I attach a copy herewith.

I have the honour to be, etc.

(*Signed*) DAG HAMMARSKJOLD
Secretary-General

Letter dated 7 August 1960 from the Deputy Prime Minister of the Republic of the Congo, addressed to the Secretary-General.

I have taken careful note of your letters of 3 August. I have, however, the honour to draw your attention to the reason underlying the decision of the Government of the Congo that Dr. Bunche's mission should be escorted by representatives of that Government. We considered that, as the Government of the Republic of the Congo is responsible for the fate of the whole Congolese nation, it would scarcely be conceivable for that Government to be absent from the contacts to be established before the entry of United Nations troops into the Congolese province of Katanga. I should therefore be grateful if you would reconsider your decision on the inclusion of our representatives in the United Nations delegation to Katanga. I attach great importance to the mutual understanding and reciprocal confidence that must govern our valuable collaboration in the interest, of course, both of the Congo and the United Nations.

I have the honour to be, etc.

(*Signed*) A. GIZENGA
Deputy Prime Minister

V

Excerpt from letter from the Secretary-General, Mr. Dag Hammarskjold, dated 5 December 1960, to Mr. Kasa-Vubu, President of the Republic of the Congo (Leopoldville).

In this connection may I be permitted to note that Mr.

Lumumba and others who recently have been seized and are now detained are members of one or the other chamber of Parliament. According to available information, persons in that position may not be prosecuted or arrested in any penal matter without prior compliance with the parliamentary procedures provided in Article 66 of the fundamental law on the structures of the Congo. You will in this context, regarding the exception made in that article for arrest in *le cas de flagrant délit*, note the interpretation given to that formula according to universal principles of law. Inasmuch as the principle of parliamentary immunity exists throughout the world as a means of protecting not the private interests of the individual but rather the structure of parliamentary democracy, world public opinion will be certain to give to this point great attention, without regard to the political positions of the various personages detained.

It has been widely noted with appreciation that you have pronounced yourself in favour of an amicable and nation wide settlement of the Congolese political crisis, to embrace all the leading political figures including, according to reported public statements by you, Mr. Lumumba. I am sure that you are in a better position than I am to evaluate the full significance for such a solution of any action taken in the present case.

Cable dated 7 December 1960 from the President of the Republic of the Congo (Leopoldville) addressed to the Secretary-General of the United Nations.

My letter of today's date deals in passing with the problem caused in the country by the flight of Mr. Lumumba and by the responsibility of O.N.U.C.* for the difficulties which have resulted.

In this connection, I would remind you of all the notes and cables of protest sent to you when the local officials of O.N.U.C. decided to provide such protection to Mr. Lumumba as virtually to shield him from the prosecution

* United Nations Organisation in the Congo.

lawfully initiated against him by the judiciary. All those remonstrations have proved futile. The attitude of the United Nations in this matter has not revealed any desire to understand the position of the Congolese authorities. It has created a very deep resentment throughout the country towards the United Nations officials; the regrettable incidents of 22 and 23 November last were the most significant and the most serious evidence of that resentment.

In view of its unwillingness to alter its position regarding the protection of Mr. Lumumba, the United Nations cannot now evade responsibility for the consequences of his escape. It was not possible for O.N.U.C. which prevented the arrest of Mr. Lumumba on pretexts totally devoid of any legal basis, not to be concerned with keeping him under surveillance, as it is now saying. If that was the case, its conduct can only be condemned as unilateral and biased, for to admit that it could obstruct justice and at the same time allow an accused person under its protection to continue his nefarious and subversive activities is unthinkable. I hope that the arrest of Mr. Lumumba in Kasai is now permanently closing a chapter in which the United Nations has certainly not helped to restore order and calm in the territory of the Republic. I venture to think that henceforth a clearer conception of the role of the United Nations in maintaining order in the Congo will prevent the recurrence of such situations, and that the system of unwarranted protection will be ended for all time.

Only in that way, Mr. Secretary-General, will it be possible to establish fruitful and effective collaboration between O.N.U.C. and the Congolese authorities, a collaboration which everyone hopes will have the most beneficial effects.

I have the honour to be, etc.

(*Signed*) JOSEPH KASA-VUBU
President of the Republic of the Congo

POSTSCRIPT

THE massacre of Patrice Lumumba by tribesmen marks a new phase in the Congo turmoil. That he was the stormy petrel of the whole tragedy is generally accepted, and while there is no justification for his murder, his permanent removal from the Congo scene, contrary to general opinion, may help unification. There is, of course, more than an equal chance that it will provide an added fillip to civil war.

The formation of the new Congolese Central Government by Kasavubu, with Ileo as Prime Minister, and the death of Lumumba are too close together in time for political comfort. Any chance the Ileo Government has of survival must undoubtedly be affected seriously by the Lumumba massacre, inasmuch as it establishes a very unfortunate and dangerous precedent in so young a nation.

The United Nations' position is assuredly worsened for the question can be asked: "What is the United Nations achieving in the political field in the Congo?" The only honest answer at the moment is, "Nothing". This opinion is strengthened by a letter addressed to Hammarskjold by a group of ten Afro-Asian nations on February 10. In it they averred that the death of Lumumba would have "the gravest consequences for the Congo and for the future of the United Nations in the Congo".

The most serious aspect of Lumumba's death is the danger that it may lead to international conflict. When the news broke, the Russians lost no time in charging that the escape and subsequent massacre were planned by the

Belgian colonialists. The unhappy thought that it was planned cannot be disregarded. Whatever the cause, the event has within it the most explosive international elements, and at the time this book goes to press one can only hope that it emerges into a world less strife-ridden than it is as I write.

M. N. HENNESSY

Bedford, New York
13 February, 1961

SOME SUGGESTIONS FOR FURTHER READING

Bartlett, Vernon. *Struggle for Africa*, Frederick A. Praeger, New York, 1953.

Bowles, Chester. *Africa's Challenge to America*, University of California Press, 1956.

Cloete, Stuart. *The African Giant*, Houghton Mifflin Company, Boston, 1955.

Considine, John J. *Africa—World of New Men*, Dodd, Mead and Company, New York, 1955.

Davidson, Basil. *The African Awakening*, The Macmillan Company, New York, 1955.

Gunther, John. *Inside Africa*, Hamish Hamilton, 1955.

Haines, C. Grove. *Africa Today*, Johns Hopkins Press, Baltimore, 1955.

Keith, A. B. *The Belgian Congo and the Berlin Act*, Clarendon Press, 1919.

Rappoport, A. S. *Life of Leopold II*, Sturgis and Walton, 1910.

Ritner, Peter. *The Death of Africa*, The Macmillan Company, New York, 1960.

Wack, H. W. *The Story of the Congo Free State*, Putnam, 1905.

Wallbank, T. W. *Contemporary Africa*, Van Nostrand, New York, 1956.

INDEX

Date Due

MAR 5 '63			
MAR 1 9 '63			
APR 2 '63			
MAR 24 '66			
APR 6 '66			
OCT 10 '66			
APR 21 '70			
MAY 5 '78			
FE 27 '80			
		PRINTED IN U. S. A.	